PRAISE FOR Follow My Lead

One of the hallmarks of Bill Bright's life was his utter dependence on the Holy Spirit. To those who say the Spirit-filled life was "just a Bill Bright thing," I say you're missing out on the greatest adventure in life. If Bill were still with us today he would heartily endorse Holly's call to become more attentive to the voice of the Holy Spirit in our everyday encounters.

Vonette Bright
Co-founder, Campus Crusade for Christ

Holly's stories make waking in the power of the Holy Spirit attainable and practical for every believer. The reflection and application questions at the end of each chapter are incredibly powerful in their ability to help readers process the challenges and encouragement each story presents. The impacting stories contained in this book are like a catapult that can launch a complacent Christian into becoming one that can boldly change the world with the gospel.

Nancy Kaser
Co-founder and co-director of Promise Child

With sensitivity toward young adults, and students in particular, Holly explores the spiritual longings of our hearts. She is a fresh and bold example of loving people wherever they are at and courageously pointing them to Christ. We need more women like her mentoring, serving and communicating to the next generation.

Shirin Taber
Author of *Wanting All the Right Things*

Follow My Lead illustrates beautifully a life surrendered to the power of the Holy Spirit and practically teaches how to live a life of daily dependence. It is a fresh look at the role of the Holy Spirit in the believer's daily life through honest, rich stories and Scripture. It will challenge, instruct and bless any who would desire a life focused on Jesus and empowered by the Spirit.

David Martinelli
Executive National Director, Campus Field Ministries for Campus Crusade for Christ

D0109415

In Holly Melton's new book, *Follow My Lead*, you will find practical and encouraging teaching on how the Holy Spirit speaks to us and leads us today. Holly writes from the perspective of one who walks close to the Lord and experiences what she teaches. A veteran staff member with Cru (Campus Crusade for Christ), Holly comes from a solid evangelical and biblical perspective on the person and work of the Holy Spirit. I highly recommend *Follow My Lead* to anyone who wants to experience a practical and biblical theology of the Spirit's work in his or her life.

J. P. Jones
Senior Pastor of Crossline Church, Adjunct Professor of Theology at
Biola University and author of *Facing Goliath*.

Holly's passion for the Lord and the lost is contagious. When I first heard her evangelism encounter I was hanging on every word. I dare you to read *Follow My Lead*—you won't be the same when you are finished. Holly is a prime example of how just one willing vessel, ready to be used by God, can mightily change the life of a soul for eternity. May God bless this publication and use it for His glory.

Trish Ramos
Cast of *The Way of the Master* TV program and
founder of FishWithTrish.com

A powerful legacy from Bill Bright has equipped believers to tell people about Jesus and to live in the power of the Holy Spirit. Holly Melton has brought these life-changing truths together through captivating stories of lives being changed. If you ever wished you could connect with others—sharing the message of forgiveness in Christ—with confidence and compassion, *Follow My Lead* will show you how. And you will love the stories!

Judy Douglass
Author, speaker, encourager; director, Women's Resources for Cru Global

"Follow me," states Jesus. It is a command that is as profoundly difficult now as it was for the first followers of Christ. As Holly reminds us, we cannot follow Jesus without listening to the same Spirit that guided Him. Through engaging stories and personal insight, *Follow My Lead* introduces us to the Spirit in fresh and surprising ways and paves the way to follow Christ.

Tim Muehlhoff, Ph.D.
Professor of Communication, Biola University;
author of *Authentic Communication: Christian Speech Engaging Culture*

follow My lead

RESPONDING TO
GOD'S VOICE
IN EVERYDAY ENCOUNTERS

Holly A. Melton

Regal

For more information and
special offers from Regal Books, email us at
subscribe@regalbooks.com

Published by Regal
From Gospel Light
Ventura, California, U.S.A.
www.regalbooks.com
Printed in the U.S.A.

Library of Congress Cataloging-in-Publication Data

Melton, Holly A.
Follow my lead : responding to God's voice in everyday encounters / Holly A. Melton.
pages cm
Includes bibliographical references and index.
ISBN 978-0-8307-6702-1 (trade paper : alk. paper) 1. Witness bearing (Christianity)
2. Evangelistic work. 3. Holy Spirit.
I. Title.
BV4520.M45 2013
248.4--dc23
2013009327

Rights for publishing this book outside the U.S.A. or in non-English languages are administered by Gospel Light Worldwide, an international not-for-profit ministry. For additional information, please visit www.glww.org, email info@glww.org, or write to Gospel Light Worldwide, 1957 Eastman Avenue, Ventura, CA 93003, U.S.A.

Cover and Interior Design by Rob Williams

To order copies of this book and other Regal products in bulk quantities,
please contact us at 1-800-446-7735.

This book is dedicated to Christy, the vampire.
My encounter with Christy taught me how to
follow God's lead, and for that I am forever grateful!

Contents

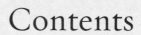

Foreword

As a traveling speaker since 1961 with Campus Crusade for Christ International, I have a passion to effectively reach the next generation with the truth and love of Jesus Christ. Although the world changes with each passing generation (culturally, socially, economically), the gospel message remains the same.

More than 60 years ago Dr. Bill Bright, founder of Campus Crusade for Christ International, authored two key booklets. *The 4 Spiritual Laws* is a concise and simple four-point outline that has been used to lead millions to receive Jesus Christ as Lord and Savior. *The Spirit-Filled Life* was written to show every believer the importance walking daily in the power of the Holy Spirit so the Lord can work powerfully both in and through his or her life.

In *Follow My Lead*, Holly Melton combines these two critical messages with practical teaching to help you discern the direction of the Holy Spirit as you engage with others in spiritual conversations. Hearing the Spirit as He directs your conversation with others will naturally bring the conversation to Jesus in such a way that it will cause others to respond.

Holly shares her own stories of Spirit-led interactions with her neighbors, a professor, students and even a madam. Each story is written to help you learn how to pray specifically for the Spirit's guidance in every situation, to know that you are following the Spirit (or taking your own direction), and to give you peace in knowing that you are being obedient to His direction—even though the outcome might not have been what you had hoped for.

Holly A. Melton

At the end of each chapter Holly summarizes the principles, asks practical and thought-provoking questions, and even suggests how you can have an ongoing dialogue with the Holy Spirit during your conversations.

Follow My Lead will give confidence to the young and old alike to share Christ with others. You will find joy and confidence as you develop relationships and share Christ! In Dr. Bright's own words, evangelism is "taking the initiative to share Christ in the *power of the Holy Spirit* and leaving the results to God."

Many books today emphasize the importance of apologetics or how to ask questions in spiritual conversations. *Follow My Lead* provides a critical component for effective evangelism to occur regardless of your situation: how to listen to the voice of the Holy Spirit. This crucial component cannot be left out if you are to continue to trust God to reach the nations with the gospel.

Until the whole world hears,
Josh D. McDowell

Introduction

We see the brokenness of lives all around us. We want to enter in and offer hope, but we don't know where to start the conversation. If we want to see the power of the gospel transform lives around us, we must learn what it means to follow the leading of the Holy Spirit.

We can learn various methods on how to share our faith; and though beneficial, this is not enough. To reach this generation with the gospel, we must learn how to listen to the wisdom given by the Holy Spirit on how to communicate the gospel uniquely to each person who comes across our path.

For the past 14 years, while serving with Cru (formally Campus Crusade for Christ), some interesting people have come across my path . . . like the woman who thought she was a vampire, the madam who oversaw prostitutes around the country, and the female professor who taught in one of the most prominent universities in the Middle East. These are just some of the stories I will share with you so that you can better see how to follow His lead in the encounters the Lord brings to you.

My heart's desire is to help people learn how to become more like Jesus and how to share Him with others. I strongly believe that the link to living out these two things is in learning how to be filled with the same Spirit that filled Jesus—to walk in the same guidance of the Spirit that led Jesus, and listen to the same wisdom of the Spirit that Jesus listened to. To that end, this book focuses on the Holy Spirit, so that through learning more about how

He leads and empowers us, you can become more like Christ and bring glory to God the Father by sharing Jesus with others.

Each chapter in *Follow My Lead* enters into a personal story as a means of coaching you on how to listen to the voice of God to bring Jesus into the conversation with others. The chapters end with reflection points, questions to ponder and even suggestions on what to pray to help you respond to God's voice and engage in spiritual conversations with those around you.

The Holy Spirit wants to show us how to connect the gospel to the people around us, if we will just *follow His lead*.

Preface

So, What *Do* We Need to Know About the Holy Spirit?

Before we dive into stories and application, let's first take a look at some basic truths about the Holy Spirit. Rather than go into heady theology, I will touch briefly on the big picture of how the Trinity works and on a few of the roles of the Holy Spirit. In no way does this explanation provide an all-encompassing view of the Holy Spirit.

The Holy Spirit is part of the Trinity: God the Father, God the Son (Jesus), and God the Holy Spirit. Each person of the Godhead plays a specific role in our salvation. As we connect which role the Father, the Son and the Holy Spirit play in our lives, we will see how to better worship the triune God, pray to the triune God and engage with the triune God in our daily interactions with others. We see the Trinity's specific roles expressed in 2 Corinthians 13:14: "The *grace* of the Lord Jesus Christ and the *love* of God and the *fellowship* of the Holy Spirit be with you all" (emphasis added).

We receive *grace* through Jesus. When Jesus died on the cross, He took God's entire wrath for your and my sin upon Himself so that we do not need to ever experience the wrath of God, but only

His love, *if* we believe in Him. Through Jesus' grace, we are reconciled to God the Father. As we gradually continue to grasp the depth of His grace, our hearts will grow in deep gratitude for this grace that we do not deserve.

Thank Jesus for taking your place, humbly realizing His willingness to surrender His life so that you can have new life through Him.

God the Father *loves* us with an undying, all-encompassing love. We see this in His willingness to send His one and only Son, Jesus, to earth, allowing Him to die in our place so that we can have a personal relationship with Him. As we continue to grasp more of His perfect love for us, we are humbled and equipped to better love, forgive and extend grace to others.

Thank the Father for His incomprehensible love for us. Ask Him to continue to reveal His love to you so that you can experience the fullness of Him in your life.

The Holy Spirit has been given to us as a means of experiencing *fellowship* with the triune God. That is, the Holy Spirit is the part of the Godhead that personally interacts with us. He is the voice we hear when God speaks to us. He is the wisdom we receive from God's Word. He is the helper in our time of need. He is our comforter in times of grief. He is the one who increases our faith. He empowers us to overcome our flesh. He gives us the courage and the words to say to make Jesus known. He guides us on how to live this life for God's glory. When we pray to God to enter into our lives, situations and conversations, we are inviting the Holy Spirit to intimately engage with us, and us with Him.

The Holy Spirit also plays a significant role in convicting us of our sin. After Jesus ascended into heaven, He sent the Holy Spirit to us to convict us of our sin (both unbeliever and believer) and to draw us to Christ, and then to empower us to be His witnesses to others.

> It is to your advantage that I go away, for if I do not go away, the Helper will not come to you. But if I go, I will send him to you. And when he comes, he will convict the world concerning sin and righteousness and judgment. . . . When

the Spirit of truth comes, he will guide you into all the truth, for he will not speak on his own authority, but whatever he hears he will speak, and he will declare to you the things that are to come. He will glorify me, for he will take what is mine and declare it to you (John 16:7-8,13-14).

The Holy Spirit dwells in us the moment we acknowledge Christ as Lord and Savior in our minds and hearts. This gives us great confidence that when we believe in Jesus, we are given the Spirit of God within us. The apostle Paul wrote about this: "In him you also, when you heard the word of truth, the gospel of your salvation, and believed in him [Jesus], were sealed with the promised Holy Spirit" (Eph. 1:13). This is the same Spirit that raised Jesus from the dead. We have the same power of God within us!

The Holy Spirit empowers us to be Jesus' witnesses and to boldly share the gospel with others: "But you will receive power when the Holy Spirit has come upon you, and you will be my witnesses in Jerusalem and in all Judea and Samaria, and to the end of the earth" (Acts 1:8). That's what happened to the Early Church: "And when they had prayed, the place in which they were gathered together was shaken, and they were all filled with the Holy Spirit and continued to speak the word of God with boldness" (Acts 4:31).

Most of the focus of this book is on this final role of the Holy Spirit and how He can empower us to be bold witnesses for Him. He is the one pursuing lives around us. He is the one who will convict people of sin and their need for a Savior. He is the one who will open their eyes to the truth of the gospel and change their lives. But what's so wonderful is that He uses us in the process, and He invites us to participate when we follow His lead.

Part One

Responding to His Voice

Therefore, as the Holy Spirit says,
"Today, if you hear his voice, do not harden your hearts."
HEBREWS 3:7-8

Hearing God's voice is not as mysterious as you may think. The Holy Spirit wants to lead you and guide you throughout each day. If He desires that you follow His lead in everyday encounters with others, then His voice must be something you can clearly hear to obey. Often, the problem is that you and I just aren't tuned in to listen for His voice.

The next nine chapters are stories intended to help you explore various ways the Holy Spirit may speak to you and through you. I hope that after reading the stories and taking some time at the end of each chapter to reflect on how the Spirit may be speaking to you, you will be encouraged to more confidently follow His lead in everyday encounters

The Vampire Who Changed My Life

Yes, that's right . . . a vampire changed my life. No, it wasn't Edward from Twilight. It was a girl I met one night on a boardwalk, who truly believed she was a vampire.

I don't know about you, but I had never met a vampire before. So, when this girl came up to me and said, "I'm a vampire. Are you afraid of me?" I didn't quite know what to say. I mean, it's not every day that someone walks up to you and starts talking about being a vampire.

Without thinking, I tilted my head and replied, "I don't know. I've never met one!"

She responded, "Well, will you talk with one?"

I shrugged nonchalantly, as if vampires approach me every day, and said, "Sure. Why not? What's your name, anyway?"

"Christy," she replied. "Christy the vampire."

It was a summer night on the boardwalk of Ocean City, New Jersey. I had just finished my junior year of college and was spending the summer with a bunch of college students, learning how to follow Jesus and share Him with others. There was a group of us

Holly A. Melton

hanging out that evening, singing worship songs—just the kind of environment you'd think a vampire would want to join in on.

Christy appeared to be a couple of years older than me, probably in her mid-twenties. She had dyed black hair, black fingernails (not the style back then), black lips, and she was wearing a Marilyn Manson T-shirt. Although Christy had approached me to talk, she wasn't saying anything. She just sat there, gazing into the waves.

I prayed a quick little prayer, asking God to give me wisdom in this strange situation. Then I thought to ask, "So, what makes one a vampire?" I figured the least I could do is learn what she thought made her a vampire.

She looked at me with dull brown eyes and said, "I participate in rituals where we sacrifice animals and then drink their blood. This is believed to help cleanse us of all impurities." Showing me her wrists, scarred with cut marks, she continued to explain, "I've tried to kill myself three times. Each time, though blood was flowing from my veins, I couldn't seem to die. I believe this means that I'm immortal. I cannot die."

As if that wasn't enough to convince me that she was a "real" vampire, she claimed, "Also, my eyes are more sensitive to the light. So I just sleep during the day and stay up all night."

I looked at her. She was serious. Only one word escaped my lips: "Interesting."

Finding Common Ground with a Vampire

I wasn't quite sure what to do about this bizarre information she had just shared with me. She was the one who approached me. Yet, I was the one asking the questions. I wondered to myself, *How do I go deeper with a person who thinks she's a vampire?* Immediately, as if the Holy Spirit opened my mouth, I asked her, "Christy, what brings you significance in your life?"

Her eyes grew big and thoughtful. She answered in a bit less of a monotone voice, "I have brought 30 women into becoming vampires with me. These women had no true friends or real family. Now they have a community where they are accepted."

I was astounded by her answer. It revealed her heart for people who were hurt and for their need for community. More than that, I was elated, for I, too, valued coming alongside women to help them find and develop a community where they could be known and loved. Christy and I had something in common. I knew that this common ground, this shared passion, was the bridge I needed to relate to her.

I smiled and affirmed Christy. "That is so wonderful—how you see the needs of these women and desire to help them. I am sure they feel quite loved by you and are thankful for the environment of community you've created."

She smiled back at me. That gave me the confidence I needed to risk continuing on and addressing the partial truths she was embracing. "You know, I've never thought of this before, probably because I've never met a vampire, but when you sacrifice animals and believe that drinking their blood is necessary, you are partially right. I, too, believe that the shedding of blood, and ultimately the death of a sacrifice, is necessary for us to be made clean."

The Holy Spirit had just opened my spiritual eyes to see how these rituals are part of the complete picture of what Jesus did as our perfect sacrifice on the cross. He allowed His blood to be shed on our behalf. But I didn't mention this parallel just yet. I continued to validate her partial truths.

"Christy, I also agree that people are immortal, and that even after this life, there is an eternity out there where we will either be with the God who gave us life, or separated from this God for all eternity. I think you are very wise to see that we were each created to live in community. The hard part is finding a community where we can be fully known and fully loved. Do you agree?"

Christy nodded, seemingly surprised how readily I was embracing her beliefs as a vampire; but I didn't stop there.

With a breath of prayer on my lips, asking for wisdom, I transitioned into the goriest presentation of the gospel I'd ever heard, let alone shared. A specific Scripture verse had instantly come to my mind, though I don't remember ever memorizing it: "Indeed, under the law almost everything is purified with blood, and without the shedding of blood there is no forgiveness of sins" (Heb. 9:22).

Christy listened intently. I went on, "We are all under the law. The law says that we are to be perfect. But we know we cannot obtain perfection on our own. Or at least, I know that I haven't been able to!"

I laughed, and continued, "Jesus was the only person who ever lived that was perfect. That is why Jesus, and only Jesus, could be the final sacrifice. He was called the Lamb, sent by God the Father to be slaughtered so that we can have a relationship with God on this side of eternity. No other animals need to be sacrificed, because Jesus paid for all of our sins—past, present and future—when He died. Jesus' blood had to be shed so that His blood could cover us. His blood is what forever cleanses us. If we believe He is the ultimate sacrifice, we will be forgiven for our wrong ways. We will be connected to God for all of eternity.

"Until we are with Him in heaven, He has placed in our souls a desire for intimate community here on earth. I believe that the most intimate community happens to those who know and accept Jesus as their final, perfect sacrifice."

At the end of explaining the gospel in this most unique way, I swallowed hard, looked intensely into her eyes and said, "Do you want to accept Jesus as your final sacrifice and invite Him into your life for all of eternity?"

I was nervous, yet full of anticipation. I knew it hadn't been me speaking, but the Holy Spirit in and through me. To my surprise and disappointment, Christy looked back at me and shook her head no. Apparently, she wasn't ready to make that faith jump yet.

I glanced at my watch and realized we had been talking for almost three hours. It was two o'clock in the morning! "Wow, Christy! It's late. Maybe we should meet up again in the morning, if you want to talk more."

She looked at me and nodded. Then she asked, "Can you drive me home? The buses have stopped running this late at night."

I didn't think it would be wise to take her home by myself, so two of my friends came with me to drive her home.

Knock, Knock, Knocking on Heaven's Door

We drove on the highway toward Christy's home, in silence. Suddenly, Christy started to knock on the window in a steady, repetitive slow knock. Knock. Knock. Knock. It was quite creepy, actually. I thought maybe she had been doing drugs, or maybe she was even possessed. I turned around from the front seat to look back at her. I asked why she was knocking on the window. She said, "I feel like something is knocking at my heart."

The verse in Revelation 3:20 leapt to my mind: "Behold, I stand at the door and knock. If anyone hears my voice and opens the door, I will come in."

I shared that verse with her and said, "I think the knocking is Jesus, and He wants you to let Him into your life."

She then replied, "I feel like I am hungry and thirsty for something, but I don't know what."

I didn't exactly remember the verse in the book of John about Jesus being the bread of life, and whoever comes to Him and believes in Him shall not hunger or thirst. But I remembered a praise song I used to sing with similar words: "I want to thirst no more. I want to hunger no more. I want to know that Jesus is my Lord." I told her these words.

She asked, "Will you sing it for me?"

I was thinking, *It's 2:30 AM! No one can sing at 2:30 in the morning!* But I tried to sing it to her anyway.

When I stopped singing, she spoke with great urgency, "Pull over right now! I need to accept Jesus in case I die before we get home!"

I was shocked. Just a few hours earlier she had believed she was immortal; now she was instantly overwhelmed with the fear of her own death.

Although there were no other cars on the road, I pulled over. I got in the backseat with her and once again shared the main points of the gospel. I wanted to make sure she really understood what she was going to commit to.

She kept nodding her head, saying, "I know. I know. I understand. I want Jesus in my life *now*!"

So right there on the side of that deserted highway, in the wee hours of the morning, this daughter of darkness became a daughter of light. It was simply surreal, and wonderful.

She prayed, acknowledging Jesus as her final sacrifice, and that His blood covered her sin. Then we got back on the road and drove the rest of the way to her house. As we pulled into the small trailer park, I said to her, "If this decision you made tonight is real, we should get together tomorrow at noon to talk about what this really means for your life."

She opened the car door, smiled and said, "I'll be there."

As we were backing out of her driveway, I noticed an old blue Dodge sitting in the driveway. The bumper caught my eye as the car lights glimmered off of a fish symbol. Someone in her family must be a Christian. Interesting . . .

Yesterday, I Was a Vampire

The next afternoon, I watched Christy walk up to me wearing the same Marilyn Manson T-shirt and the same black lipstick, but something had drastically changed . . . her eyes. They were glimmering, sparkling. And a smile that could not be erased was on her lips. Still about 20 feet away, she picked up her pace and yelled, "Holly! Holly! Can you teach me how to share Jesus with others like you did with me last night?!"

My first thought was, *Wow! Even believers don't want to learn how to share their faith! Here is this brand-new believer, ecstatic to learn how to share Jesus with others*. I didn't remember exactly what I shared with her the night before. It was such an unusual conversation. So I suggested we go on the boardwalk and find someone to talk with about God and see what the Holy Spirit would do.

We approached a 13-year-old boy, who said his name was Mark, and struck up a conversation. As we started to talk about spiritual things, he asked a really good question: "How do you know you're different when you become a Christian?"

Not being big on theology in college, I took a moment to think about how to answer that with my own testimony. Christy, thinking faster than me, jumped right in ahead of me and said, "Well, yesterday I was a vampire, but today I'm a born-again Christian, and boy do I feel the difference!"

The boy's eyes got huge as she proceeded to share the gospel with him in the same gory fashion I had done with her the night before. She looked him right in the eyes and with all seriousness said, "Death is necessary. Blood is essential. We are made for community. We are immortal. But we must trust in Jesus' sacrifice of His own life on our behalf so that we can live forever in community with God and others who believe in Him."

I was shocked by how much she had remembered from the night before. It was almost word for word the crazy presentation I had given her just shy of 12 hours before. At the end of her explanation, this young teenager prayed with her, right there on the boardwalk! Again, I couldn't believe what I was experiencing. Christy hadn't even been a believer for 12 hours, yet she already led someone to Jesus! It was truly amazing.

The Gift

The story does not end here. My day job that summer was working at a small bed and breakfast, located one block from the ocean. I'd tidy up the rooms, then hang out on the front porch with the vacationers and read books. I couldn't believe I was getting paid to hang out and read on a porch, at a place that was only a block from the ocean!

One couple I met while sitting on the porch were believers. They asked me about my summer. I was excited to share the story of Christy and her changed life. I told them I was meeting with her every day to help her grow in the Lord.

"She is from a poor family and has no money. The funny thing is seeing her meet me in her goth-look wardrobe every day, excited to learn more about Jesus."

The husband smiled, shook his head, then pulled out his wallet and handed me a crisp $100 bill. He said, "She has a new life. Now she needs new clothes. Take her shopping." They were touched by her testimony and her hunger to learn, and they wanted to bless her in her newfound faith.

When I met with Christy later that day, I excitedly offered her the money so that she could buy new clothes for the "new Christy." But that wasn't what she wanted to spend the money on. She asked if we could go, instead, to the small Christian store on the boardwalk and buy Christian music. This just showed me even more how she had been transformed from the inside out. As we walked, I tried to think of popular Christian bands she might like. When we arrived at the store, she said that all she really wanted to listen to were hymns. I was humbled to see that I didn't have to worry about changing her outside appearance. God was focusing on changing her inside. What a beautiful thing to see her purchase and cherish her new music!

My two final weeks with Christy came to a close and I was truly sad to see the summer end. I had seen God work through me in ways I had never thought possible.

Miracle Encounters

As I was waiting at my gate in the Philadelphia airport to head home, a woman sat down beside me. Noticing my Christian T-shirt, she smiled and asked, "Are you a Christian?"

"Yes," I said. "You?"

"Yup! What brought you to New Jersey?"

Since we still had half an hour until boarding, I shared with her about the summer and the amazing story of "Christy, the vampire." She then asked me to wait a minute as she went to get her husband. When she brought him over, he introduced himself as the pastor of a church in Ocean City, and he wanted to hear my story about Christy.

When I finished, he shot his head up, looked into my eyes and said, "You're not going to believe this, but Christy's father goes to our church. We've been praying for her for the past five years. She's not wanted to talk to any believers, so we've simply been praying that God would somehow work a miracle in her life."

I sat there, stunned. An entire church body had been praying for Christy for five years.

I looked at him, speechless, a tear streaming down my face while he continued, "Now that we know she's a believer, we will talk with her and hopefully get to continue discipling her."

I couldn't believe it. There I was, sitting in an airport, minding my own business, when this woman approached me and struck up a conversation. I learned they had been praying for Christy for *years* and wanted to disciple her. This was truly a miraculous encounter! As I continued to ponder it, I realized that my encounter with Christy on the beach was also a miracle. I had witnessed a girl go from darkness to light and then lead someone else to the Lord. Now I was seeing how the Lord was truly bringing her into the community she so desired. The gospel was being powerfully played out before my eyes.

On the flight home, wouldn't you know it, this couple sat right in front of me. As I looked out the window and saw New Jersey getting smaller and smaller, until the cloud cover made it disappear altogether, I knew I was forever changed. I thought I was going to be a lawyer. That had been my plan for my life since the fourth grade. I thought that was my passion. But during the summer, that one encounter—that one changed life—showed me that God had a greater purpose for my life: *to see lives transformed with the gospel.*

From that time on, I've wanted to do nothing else with my life but learn how to be open to whomever the Holy Spirit wants to put on my path. I want to see the incredible happen before my eyes. Seeing lives changed by the gospel became my new passion, my new direction that summer of my junior year. And it can become your passion and direction too.

I later learned that Christy went back to her coven of vampires and started to share Jesus with the women she had previously brought into that community. She was able to share the gospel with 12 of them before the head vampire got word of what she was doing and tried to take Christy's life. She escaped, and the pastor and his wife took her in, becoming her new family. This new community of believers protected her, and she began to grow even more in her faith.

Two Changed Lives

Christy, a former vampire, was changed by the power of the gospel, and she forever changed me as well. Her transformed life transformed mine. She showed me that the Holy Spirit could take a person who is so far away from God and draw her close to Him in an instant. He can give you and me the right words to share even when we are talking to someone we have no clue how to relate to. He can open a person's eyes to the truth on a dark road. He can help him or her grasp enough of the gospel, overnight, that he or she can share it with others the next day.

When I was a little kid, the gospel transformed my life. I knew Jesus loved me, and when I invited Him into my life, I knew He'd be with me forever. That encounter with Christy was a different transformation, a different revelation. I saw how God wanted to use me. It had begun as just an ordinary evening at the beach. I was in my own little world when He decided to bring Christy to me so that, through me, He could make Himself known to her. My ordinary night became extraordinary as I saw the secrets and strategies of heaven unfold as this one life changed before my eyes. I was a part of a divine appointment. And this divine appointment didn't just change my life, or Christy's life, but every life that Christy has touched thereafter.

MOMENT OF REFLECTION

*But the Helper, the Holy Spirit, whom the Father will
send in my name, he will teach you all things and bring to
your remembrance all that I have said to you. Peace I leave
with you; my peace I give to you. Not as the world gives do I
give to you. Let not your hearts be troubled,
neither let them be afraid.*

JOHN 14:26-27

Holly A. Melton

As I reflect on this experience, I see how the Holy Spirit entered in and taught me things I hadn't understood before:

- *The Holy Spirit may want us to engage someone with whom we think we have nothing in common* (see 1 Cor. 9:19-22). I had no clue that I could find similarities between me and a woman who thought she was a vampire. God wanted to show me differently. I had to be willing to trust the Holy Spirit for how to engage her attention in order to find some sort of common ground. My first response could easily have been to be turned off by her appearance and approach. Yet, I was willing to sit down, take the time and talk with her.

- *We can begin the conversation by learning about the other person. What matters most to the person? What does she live for? What brings him significance in life* (see 1 Cor. 10:24)? I needed to learn why Christy thought she was a vampire. I needed to hear a little of her story. I wanted to learn what she cared about. I also wanted to find a way to relate to her even though our lives seemed so vastly different from each other's. Realizing that we both cared about hurting women helped us feel more connected to each other, emphasizing our similarities rather than our differences.

- *People believe partial truths all the time. We can ask the Holy Spirit to help us connect them to the whole truth* (see John 8:32). As I listened to Christy share about being a vampire, I saw glimmers of truth in what she was saying. I first affirmed how she was seeing the value of those things, even if she wasn't grasping the whole truth. This helped her see that I was for her and not against her. She was seeking good things (cleansing and community), and I wanted to be a part of affirming where she was on her journey.

- *The Holy Spirit may show us how to share the gospel in a way we have never thought of before* (see Acts 17:22-31). I knew it

wasn't enough to affirm the partial truths Christy currently believed. She needed to hear the whole truth. I had
no clue how to contextualize the gospel to a vampire, but
I asked the Holy Spirit to show me, and He did. I had never
shared the gospel like that before, and I never have since. I
believe that's how God prefers it—for us to depend on Him
regarding each circumstance and every individual person.

• *Even when we have little or no experience, the Holy Spirit can
greatly use us to affect people's lives* (see 1 Cor. 1:27). We should
never think that God can't use us in a situation. God gave
us the Holy Spirit as our Helper so that we do not need to
fear our inadequacies. When we start to learn how to ask
the Spirit to enter into our conversations, we will begin to
see how He is willing to use even the young and inexperi-
enced as long as we are willing to trust Him.

• *God the Father has sent us the Helper so that we do not need to be
afraid of people, and we can walk in peace in those situations* (see
Ps. 118:6; 2 Tim. 1:7). When the Holy Spirit is guiding us, we
have nothing to fear. When He is the one giving us the questions or the next steps in the conversation, we do not need
to worry about the outcome. There is tremendous peace in
knowing that the Holy Spirit is in control of every conversation. The words I say, therefore, are not based on my own
wisdom or experience. Thank You, God!

• *The Holy Spirit can bring Scripture to mind that can specifically re-
late to the person(s) with whom we are engaging* (see Acts 28:22-
28). In order for this to happen, we must study the Word of
God to let it sink into our hearts and minds. Even though
I hadn't memorized the passages I shared with Christy, I
had read them multiple times as I've read through the
Bible; so the Holy Spirit was able to bring them to mind.
Being in the Word powerfully equips us to be used by the
Holy Spirit in people's lives.

Questions to Ponder

1. Who is in your world that you have no idea how to relate to? How can you begin learning more about this person (or persons)?
2. When you think about what people around you believe, what is partially true about their beliefs? How might you be able to affirm those things that are partially true and help connect them to the whole truth?
3. What lies come to mind about your own fears or inadequacies when you are given an opportunity to talk about spiritual things with others? How can you fight those lies with the truth?

Conversation with God

1. Ask the Holy Spirit to show you how to enter into a conversation and learn about a person with whom you don't naturally relate.
2. In the moment, ask the Holy Spirit to give you the wisdom to know the questions to ask and the discernment to see the partial truths the person believes.
3. Ask the Holy Spirit to show you connections to what a person believes, and how you can share Jesus with him or her.
4. Ask the Holy Spirit to work through you in the lives of others.

Chapter 2

Being a Freshman Stinks!

All we like sheep have gone astray; we have turned—every one—to his own way; and the LORD has laid on him the iniquity of us all.
ISAIAH 53:6

Because I grew up in a small town, and in a Christian home, most of my social group during high school was made up of the youth group at church. Though every youth group has its drama, it wasn't until I went off to college that my heart was opened to the deep struggles and pain my peers were experiencing.

There was only one thing I prayed for my senior year of high school: my future roommate. Little did I know that in my first home away from home, at the University of Arizona, I would be sharing a room with a girl named Shanequa. During the first week of school, Shanequa asked me out of the blue, "What is your view of homosexuals?"

I looked at her, feeling a little shocked, and said, "They are people who deserve to be loved and valued. I do believe that participating in the act of homosexuality is a sin, but it is not any worse of a sin than other sins people commit. Your identity is found in who God created you to be, not in what you do or don't do."

I don't know if it helped or hurt to be so direct on my views the first week of school, but her only reply was, "Well, I'm bisexual."

On the second week of school, her girlfriend spent the night. I didn't know what to do with this uncomfortable situation, so I prayed on my top bunk, trying to not focus on their behavior on the bottom bunk.

Many adults advised me to try to change roommates, but I had prayed specifically for my roommate. If there was one thing I was certain of, I knew the Lord wanted me to live with her. I asked the Holy Spirit to show me how to make this situation work.

One evening, Shanequa asked why I read the Bible every day. Apparently, she had been watching me and I didn't even realize it. As I shared with her about my relationship with Jesus and how reading the Bible was a way for Him to speak to me personally, she started to open up.

"You know, I was raised Jehovah's Witness. I left the church because they ignored the fact that my father was sexually abusing me. They still allowed him to stay in leadership. I *hate* men. A man abused me, and other men covered it up. I felt so alone and rejected. I didn't know whom I could trust. Then Mindy came along.

"Mindy was the first person who I felt loved and cared for me. As the friendship got more intimate, we became intertwined in a sexual relationship. I hadn't planned to fall into a sexual relationship; it just happened. I know it's wrong, and God isn't happy with me. But Mindy is the only one who has loved me. I can't imagine life without her."

Shanequa's words revealed to me that behind the attitude of a very independent, stubborn woman was a very fragile, hurting person. It was the first time my heart really broke for the lost.

To be honest with you, I must admit that sometimes when I see the way people live their lives my first thoughts are, *They seem too far from God to want to hear about Jesus.* Or, *I'm sure they love their sin and addictions too much to want to see God transform them.* Or, *They have had such a challenging life, how can the gospel really bring them comfort and hope in a tangible way?* These are faulty thoughts.

No one is too far from God's grace. Just because we see someone stuck in addiction doesn't mean he or she doesn't want to get free. When tragedy strikes and hopelessness sets in, often hearts long for someone to offer them hope.

The Residents

My heart for freshmen students continued to grow, and for my junior year I decided that the best way to stay engaged with them would be to serve as a Resident Assistant in the dorms. Again, I prayed for just one thing: the hall that I would be assigned to. I was placed in Coronado, the rowdiest coed dorm on campus.

Before the freshmen came, I prayed in every room. I prayed that I could get to know each freshman on a deeper level. I prayed that I would be a good mentor and a safe friend. And I prayed that the Holy Spirit would show me opportunities to minister to them on a spiritual level.

There was palpable excitement in the dorms that first week of school. Everyone seemed to be bouncing off the walls with energy, zipping from event to event, blaring music and chatting it up with their dorm neighbors. By the fourth week of school, the weight of classes and the exhaustion of late nights, wild parties and unmet expectations began to set in.

Knocks on my door became more frequent as students who didn't know how to cope with the stress, the peer pressure, and their new life away from home sought me out. They had a clear need for community, hope and purpose, but they didn't know where else to go or to whom they could turn. Truly, I saw this verse come to life: "They were like sheep without a shepherd" (Mark 6:34).

One morning, when I opened the Bible to read Psalm 107, the Holy Spirit gave me a fresh understanding of how the people around me could relate to that psalm. It describes four types of people: the wanderer, the prisoner, the fool and the traumatized. I saw each type of person enter my room and share his or her story. Each one cried out for help. Sadly, only some took it.

THE WANDERER

Some wandered in desert wastes, finding no way to a city to dwell in; hungry and thirsty, their soul fainted within them. Then they cried to the LORD in their trouble, and he delivered them from their distress. He led them by a straight way till they reached a city to dwell in. Let them thank the LORD for his steadfast love, for his wondrous works to the children of man! For he satisfies the longing soul, and the hungry soul he fills with good things.
PSALM 107:4-9

Psychologists consider loneliness to be the most difficult emotion for people to endure over time. This emotional state is true for more people than we commonly realize. People are wandering, seeking somewhere to belong. They feel lost in a city full of people. I had never seen so clearly how directionless people were until Jack showed up at my door.

"Holly, can I talk to you?"

"Sure, Jack. What's up?"

"Well, this is sort of uncomfortable to ask, but do you think I'm gay?"

"Huh? Why are you asking me this?"

"Well, the guys in the hall are saying I must be gay because I've asked six girls out and they've all said no. They keep suggesting that I should ask a guy out and see if he says yes. Maybe I attract men, not women."

I had never heard such logic before, but I asked the Holy Spirit to give me wisdom as I replied, "Jack, having girls say no to a date does not make you gay. It seems like you're putting a lot of pressure on yourself to get a date every weekend, when really this is a time to get to know people and make friends. Maybe you should focus on that first. You could join me and my friends when we hang out each weekend. My friends are very welcoming, and I'm sure they would love to meet you. "

"I don't know. Thanks for the offer. It just seems like this is what guys do in college. Live for the weekends. Ask a different girl out every week and try to get laid. I don't even know what finding friends would really look like."

My heart broke for Jack that day. He was a wanderer, having no clear identity of who he was or where he could belong. I continued to invite him to join me in my community of friends, but he wanted to fit in with the crowd. Finally, one day he gave in and asked a guy out. The guy said yes. By the middle of his freshmen year, Jack openly identified himself with the gay lifestyle.

Even though I continued to invite Jack to events with my friends, he chose to wander on his own path. I prayed for Jack as long as he lived on my floor; and once again my heart broke for the lost.

THE PRISONER

Some sat in darkness and in the shadow of death, prisoners in affliction and in irons, for they had rebelled against the words of God, and spurned the counsel of the Most High. So he bowed their hearts down with hard labor; they fell down, with none to help. Then they cried to the LORD in their trouble, and he delivered them from their distress. He brought them out of darkness and the shadow of death, and burst their bonds apart. Let them thank the LORD for his steadfast love, for his wondrous works to the children of man! For he shatters the doors of bronze and cuts in two the bars of iron.

PSALM 107:10-16

Tyler was another sweet guy on my floor. He was quieter than the others, but he would always hang around, just listening. I began to notice that he was very shy around women. I felt the prodding of the Spirit to ask him about it; so one day when he stopped by my room, I took the step of faith to ask, "Hey, Tyler, I just want you to know you seem like a really sweet, nice guy. I'm sure many girls on the floor would want to get to know you. But I've noticed that you seem shy around them. Have you noticed that?"

He nodded and hung his head.

"Why do you think that is? I believe the girls are missing out!"

He looked at me and said, "I don't know how to talk to girls."

I smiled, rolled my eyes playfully and responded, "Sure you do! You talk to me!"

It was his turn to roll his eyes as he said, "You're my RA. That's different."

"Well, thanks!" I joked. "I'm a girl, too, you know, even if I'm two years older."

He was quiet for a moment, and then he shifted his weight on his feet and said, "I'm addicted to porn. Bad. I have posters all over my walls in my room. I look at videos for hours each night. Those are the women I see. I have no clue how to talk to the girls in the hall after looking at those other pictures. It's like women aren't real people to me anymore. Just objects I look right through."

I could tell his heart was burdened, and he was feeling like a prisoner to his own addiction. I sat down on the side of the bed beside him and asked the Spirit to show me what to say. I decided that I would talk confidently about God without worrying if Tyler believed in God or not.

I said, "God made man and woman beautiful and naked for each other. Because of our selfish fleshly desires, over time people have warped the beauty of men and women and how we are to look at each other. And these are the effects of this distortion. We don't know how to really love each other and appreciate the beauty of the person before us without looking at him or her like an object."

Tyler nodded as he listened, his eyes glued to the floor. I asked him, "Would you like help overcoming this addiction so that you can start to engage more healthily with the women around you?"

Tyler shook his head and replied, "I don't know; let me think about it."

Tyler didn't decide he wanted to break free from being a prisoner to pornography while living on my floor, but I prayed for him that entire year. Once again, my heart broke for the lost.

THE FOOL

Some were fools through their sinful ways, and because of their iniquities suffered affliction; they loathed any kind of food, and they drew near to the gates of death. Then they cried to the LORD in their trouble, and he delivered them from their distress. He sent out his word and healed them, and delivered them from their destruction. Let them thank the LORD for his steadfast love, for his wondrous works to the children of man! And let them offer sacrifices of thanksgiving, and tell of his deeds in songs of joy.

PSALM 107:17-22

Nichole was a beautiful young woman with dark almond-shaped eyes and caramel-colored skin. The first time I entered her room to say hi and get to know her better, I was struck by the absence of people in the photo collage on her wall. Every photo was of her and her dog. I chose to start the conversation on the safe side and said, "What a cute dog! What's her name?"

Nichole's eyes glistened as she replied, "Peaches! I named her that because as a puppy she was just a ball of orange and blonde fur. I got her when I was just a little girl."

"Cute!" I turned to look at her and said, "You must miss her very much. I'm sure it was hard to leave such a cute dog behind."

"Yes. She is my life. I didn't really have any friends growing up, and my parents are always gone on cruises or vacations; so all I had at home was my little sister and Peaches. She really is my best friend."

My mind started to spin as I thought about how it sounded like Nichole had raised herself and her little sister. My heart grew with compassion. "Well, please share with me stories about Peaches anytime, okay?"

"Sure!" She smiled, and I went on to say hi to her suitemates next door.

Exactly one week later, on a Thursday evening, her suitemates came rushing to my room, frantically shouting, "It's Nichole! We think she hurt herself, but she's locked in the bathroom and won't open the door! We need you to get in and see what's wrong!"

I rushed to her room and banged on her bathroom door. Nichole was moaning on the other side. Seemingly oblivious to our pounding, she wasn't moving to open the door. I ran to get the master key and found Nichole sitting in the bathtub, bleeding. She was slumped over with both of her wrists slit, going in and out of consciousness, her eyes rolling back and forth in her head.

I immediately grabbed the white towels on the counter and pressed them to her wrists in an attempt to stop the bleeding while urgently directing the suitemates to call 911. I asked Nichole what had happened.

Not able to look at me, she slurred the words, "Peaches. She's dead."

"What?!" I exclaimed in disbelief.

"My parents called. They said she died . . . a month ago. They were on a cruise. Left her home alone. They never bothered to tell me." Then, with slow breaths between each word she said, "She . . . was . . . my . . . life."

The paramedics came just then and hurriedly whisked her away. The police entered as soon as Nichole was taken out and started searching her room. They discovered drugs in one of her drawers, as well as a wad of money. It appeared she'd been dealing drugs.

I couldn't believe it! Nichole was a sweet, beautiful girl. I had no idea she had been dealing drugs. And now to see her life shattered because of the death of her dog. I knew that even if she survived, she wouldn't be allowed to come back to the dorms, due to the drugs they found. How could I reach out to her?

A few days later, Nichole was released from the hospital. She was recovering well, but the school said that she needed to find another place to live and that she had one hour to gather her things. When I heard that, I knew I wouldn't have much time to talk to her and that it would be chaotic. I felt the prodding of the Spirit to write her a letter.

In the letter, I shared how beautiful I thought she was, how she has a purpose of being on this earth, and that God has a plan for her life. I wrote out the gospel and then gave her my address and phone number if she ever wanted to contact me.

When Nichole showed up to pack, she was accompanied by a police officer. He watched her as she packed up all of her belongings. I knew I wouldn't be able to have a deep conversation with her, so I discretely placed the letter I had written in the duffle bag on the bed. I prayed that she'd read it and call me. Sadly, that was the last day I saw her. I have no clue where she ended up or what happened to her. She never contacted me or acknowledged my letter. Once again, my heart broke for the lost.

THE TRAUMATIZED

Some went down to the sea in ships doing business on the great waters; they saw the deeds of the Lord, his wondrous works in the deep. For he commanded and raised the stormy wind, which lifted up the waves of the sea. They mounted up to heave; they went down to the depths; their courage melted away in their evil plight; they reeled and staggered like drunken men and were at their wits' end. Then they cried out to the Lord in their trouble, and he delivered them from their distress. He made the storm be still, and the waves of the sea were hushed. Then they were glad that the waters were quiet, and he brought them to their desired haven. Let them thank the Lord for his steadfast love, for his wondrous works to the children of man! Let them extol him in the congregation of the people, and praise him in the assembly of the elders.

PSALM 107:23-32

Holly A. Melton

These successful business merchants seemed to acknowledge the Lord's existence but did not cry out to Him until they were in peril at sea. Many people seem to know of God but do not engage with Him until something tragic happens. This is what happened with my friend Mark. Mark knew the Lord but chose to go his own, independent way when he arrived at college. A bear of a man with a gentle heart, Mark was the lead quarterback for our football team. He was loved by all of his teammates and had an all-around attractive personality. People wanted to be around him and be like him.

Mark was a Christian, but becoming instantly popular led him to quickly slip into the party scene, especially with regards to drinking. People remarked that he was even more fun when he was drunk, so every weekend Mark would drink up, then come home and sleep the day away.

Around 2 AM one morning, his roommate knocked on my door, waking me up. I answered the door and he declared, "Mark is losing it. He came home about an hour ago, eyes bloodshot from crying, and he's been weeping in his bed in the fetal position ever since. He won't tell me what happened, and I can't get him to stop crying."

We ran back to his room together. As soon as Mark spotted me at the door, he turned around on his bed to face the wall, still sobbing. I went over, put my hand on his shoulder and prayed for God's favor to get through to Mark.

I gently rubbed his shoulder in silence. Then, I bent over to whisper to him, "Mark, what happened? Why are you crying?"

He started to calm down, though deep heaving sobs were still trying to escape from within him. After some silence, he said, "I killed Bryce tonight. I killed Bryce!"

At that, he began to heave and sob again. Though alarmed at his comment, I wrapped my arms around him. "What do you mean, you killed Bryce?"

"I was driving, drunk. Bryce was in the front seat. I didn't see the car coming from the right side and it hit us full speed. Bryce went through the windshield. I saw it with my own eyes!

I saw him moving and struggling, and then he just stopped moving. I killed him."

I didn't have words for what happened, but I felt the Spirit prodding me to pray for him. I gently asked, "Mark, can I pray for you? I can't imagine what you are walking through right now, but God does." He nodded and I began, "Father, You know Mark. You know he loved Bryce and that his intention was not to harm his friend. Would you please come and comfort Mark right now as he wrestles through this tragedy and walks through the grief? I know You can guide him even through this storm."

Mark took a deep breath, calmer than I'd seen him yet, and he said, "I walked away from God. I put my focus on football, popularity, and having fun over loving God and loving others. I wish it hadn't come to this, for me to see how I've lost my focus."

We talked until four in the morning about the grace, love, mercy and forgiveness of God. I saw Mark humble himself and cry out to the Lord in his pain and anguish. Over time, I saw Mark heal and saw his light truly shine onto his friends.

Those Who Cry Out to the Lord

As I kept meditating on Psalm 107, I saw a theme for each person represented in the psalm. At some point, they got to a place where they cried out to the Lord. Each person who chose to cry out to the Lord experienced God's entering into their situation and healing them. He led the wanderer into community. He burst the chains off of the prisoner. He delivered the fool from destruction. He restored the traumatized from distress.

As I look back at the people God has placed around me, some have cried out to Jesus and some have not. Instead of worrying if I could have said more or done things differently, I know there is still something I can do: I can pray that the Holy Spirit will bring them to a point where they will cry out to the Lord, in surrender. This can be my continual prayer for them because I know that if they do that, then God *will* deliver them. It's His promise.

MOMENT OF REFLECTION

Now when they heard of the resurrection of the dead, some mocked. But others said, "We will hear you again about this." So Paul went out from their midst. But some men joined him and believed.
ACTS 17:32-24

· We cannot afford to live a self-focused life in our own Christian bubble. Too many people around us are living an isolated, depressing, hopeless life (see Phil. 2:3-4).

· We might not naturally get along with non-believers around us, but we can ask the Holy Spirit how to make the situation work for His glory (see Rom. 12:15-18).

· We shouldn't shy away from spending time with Jesus around non-believers, be it prayer or Bible study.

· As with Shanequa, we need to be honest and respectful when a non-believer asks our view on things that the Bible directly calls sin. The Holy Spirit is the one who will convict him or her, but we cannot water down what the Bible teaches if we want to see the Holy Spirit work in that person's life (see Col. 4:6).

· Pray over places, such as neighborhoods, office cubicles, classrooms, and the like. Prepare these places for the Spirit to work (see 2 Thess. 3:1-5).

· As with Tyler, we might observe someone's behavior and feel prodded by the Spirit to ask him or her about it. Often, people don't take the time to notice or enter into what's going on in other people's lives. That can make all the difference in becoming a trusted, safe person—which often is a good first step (see Heb. 10:22-24).

- We don't have to experience what others have experienced to engage with them. We just need to be willing to listen to them, love them, give them time to grieve, and enter into their journey alongside them. We can offer prayer for those who are in pain and grief (see Rom. 12:15-18).

- We need to learn how to become safe people by letting others be where they are at in the process. They need to feel accepted no matter how differently we view their situation or actions (see 1 Pet. 4:8).

- We need to be willing to see, acknowledge and even understand their pain, their hurts and their fears so that we can truly empathize. We need to allow them to feel their pain as well. We are not there to fix their pain, but to enter into it with them (see 1 Pet. 3:8).

Questions to Ponder

1. Are you spending all of your time in a Christian bubble, or do you engage with non-believers as well? Do you know the people who live next door? Do you know the people down the street? What can you do to initiate meeting them? How can you get to know them more deeply?

2. Do you love the sinner but hate the sin? Does your heart break for those who do not yet know Jesus personally?

3. Read Psalm 107. Who comes to mind that you can reach out to and pray for that fit into these four types of people?

4. When you hear of something painful going on in someone's life, how do you respond? Do you try to avoid it? Do you try to solve the problem? Do you try to placate it? Or do you know how to enter in, listen, empathize and pray for that person?

Conversation with God

1. Ask the Holy Spirit to open your eyes to the wanderers, the prisoners, the fools and the traumatized around you.

2. Ask the Holy Spirit to open your heart to have compassion on them.

3. Ask the Holy Spirit how you can enter into their lives and be an example of someone who loves the sinner but not the sin.

4. Ask the Holy Spirit for opportunities to share the Word of God with them, because it, alone, has the power to convict souls.

5. Ask the Holy Spirit for opportunities to pray for them and with them.

6. Ask the Holy Spirit to bring them to a place where they will cry out to the Lord in surrender, allowing Him to change their lives.

7. Thank the Lord that when they cry out to Him, He will heal them and deliver them because of His steadfast love.

Chapter 3

From One Poem to Another

Poetry deals with the heart. When we read poetry, it opens our souls to experience the depth and breadth of emotions that the writer wants us to feel. It was Angela's poem that opened my heart to her journey with men, and how it has affected her view of herself.

Angela's poetry intimately speaks of the loss of her virginity at a young age, and how she no longer believed that she was beautiful. As you read her words, try to internalize what she was feeling and experiencing as she wrote them.

Picture Perfect
Artificial love costs pieces of happiness.
The hot sweaty men are ignorant thieves
powered by a thirst for instant gratification
with no thought for the aftermath.
They steal and take till there will be nothing left.
The emptiness they leave
will destroy the beautifully shaped woman,
who's heart was once full.
As it happens, she begins to not care anymore.
She believes she was built for this.

Holly A. Melton

Her body is a machine, she convinces herself,
because machines are inhuman and unfeeling as she has become.
She was provided for them.
She's a performer on her satiny, ruffled stage.
Then her client dresses and abandons her sleeping.
Waking up disillusioned,
robbed of another piece of her soul, taken again.
The men, of course, love her when she's easy.
They await her perfect grand entrance.
She can't disappoint them.
Perfect smile, face, makeup, accessories,
charming, witty, sensual body, and skills.
Her hair gets messed up and the hangovers start.
She's ugly now and also an inconvenience.
The fast and disposable lover to men
still appears as the beautiful, talented,
well-bred daughter to her parents.
The two-faced ugliness becomes chaotic.
She's easy to show off
for the lucky man that has her on his arm.
She's easy to use, plus she's free,
and once she's out of sight, she's out of mind.
One thing that can always be counted on,
is that she leaves with less than when she came.

I met Angela when she was 18 and a freshman in college. When I asked about her accent, she told me some of her family background.

"I'm from Egypt. When I was 12, my father kidnapped me from my mother, and we fled the country after he got into a fight and killed a man. Though we are Muslim, he drank heavily and would often beat me. I remember him throwing me against the wall a couple of times as if I were a paper doll. When his friends would come over, the house was thick with the smell of booze and cigars. He wouldn't say anything when the men would take me down to the basement. I knew I had better keep my mouth shut and not scream. He'd lose face. Then I'd surely get beaten."

Holly A. Melton

"Angela!" I exclaimed in disbelief. "You lived with him up until now?!"

She shook her head and continued, "I came to school with too many bruises one time. I couldn't wear long sleeve shirts when our school had no air conditioning, so they saw my bruised arms from where men held me down. The school called child protective services and I was taken away. I was in and out of foster homes the past two years. Some weren't any better than if I had been living with my dad."

I sat there listening in horror as Angela told me her life journey. I couldn't imagine how she made it to college after all of this! I stated that, and she sadly smiled. "I may not have a soul anymore for what's been done to me, but I still have a brain. I was top of my class. Valedictorian. When I was asked to give the address at my graduation, child protective services was afraid my father would be in the crowd of the football stadium and try to kill me. I was advised to wear a bulletproof vest under my gown, just in case."

"Oh, my goodness! Angela, what a life you have lived!"

That's when she asked me if I'd want to read her poem. As I sat there and read "Picture Perfect," tears streamed down my face. Angela didn't know how beautiful she was. She didn't know she was valuable and priceless. I had no clue how I, in my sheltered life, could come alongside a young woman who had already lived such a tragic one. Not knowing how to enter into her pain, I asked the Holy Spirit to give me wisdom on how to comfort her and bring her hope.

David's Poem

Angela and I were from completely different backgrounds and faiths. She was Muslim; I was Christian. What could I say that could begin on common ground? I knew two things: We both believed in God, and she loved poetry. I asked the Holy Spirit to give me a poem we could both relate to. The poem that came to my mind was Psalm 139, written by King David. I knew that Muslims thought of David as a prophet and would value his words. Psalm 139 is about how we are fearfully and wonderfully made by God. This seemed to be exactly what Angela needed to hear.

I asked Angela if we could meet up again that evening so that I could share a poem with her, like she shared with me. She instantly perked up and said she'd love that.

I spent time that afternoon reading over the psalm and asked the Holy Spirit to show me how to relate it to her. I got the idea to write it out so that I could hand it to her and she could read it over and over again.

That evening our souls were entwined with the words David had penned to God. Sitting side by side, I read his poem out loud to her:

O Lord, you have searched me and known me!
You know when I sit down and when I rise up;
you discern my thoughts from afar.
You search out my path and my lying down
and are acquainted with all my ways.
Even before a word is on my tongue,
behold, O Lord, you know it altogether.
You hem me in, behind and before,
and lay your hand upon me.
Such knowledge is too wonderful for me;
it is high; I cannot attain it.

Where shall I go from your Spirit?
Or where shall I fall from your presence?
If I ascend to heaven, you are there!
If I make my bed in Sheol, you are there!
If I take the wings of the morning
and dwell in the uttermost parts of the sea,
even there your hand shall lead me,
and your right hand shall hold me.
If I say, "Surely the darkness shall cover me,
and the light about me be night,"
even the darkness is not dark to you;
the night is bright as the day,
for darkness is as light with you.

Holly A. Melton

For you formed my inward parts;
you knit me together in my mother's womb.
I praise you, for I am fearfully and wonderfully made.
Wonderful are your works;
my soul knows it very well.
My frame was not hidden from you,
when I was being made in secret,
intricately woven in the depths of the earth.
Your eyes saw my unformed substance;
in your book were written, every one of them,
the days that were formed for me,
when as yet there was none of them.

How precious to me are your thoughts, O God!
How vast is the sum of them!
If I would count them, they are more than the sand.
I awake, and I am still with you.

Oh that you would slay the wicked, O God!
O men of blood, depart from me!
They speak against you with malicious intent;
your enemies take your name in vain.
Do I not hate those who hate you, O Lord?
And do I not loathe those who rise up against you?
I hate them with complete hatred;
I count them my enemies.

Search me, O God, and know my heart!
Try me and know my thoughts!
And see if there be any grievous way in me,
and lead me in the way everlasting!

Fearfully and Wonderfully Made

This time it was Angela's turn to cry. She looked up at me and said,
"Is this poem true? Is it for real? Is this how God sees me?"

Holly A. Melton

Tears sprang to my eyes as I nodded and replied, "Yes, Angela. You are fearfully and wonderfully made. God knows about every moment of your life. He knows when you have felt like you were in darkness. He knows the men who harmed you and took away your innocence, and it angers Him. He is with you right now. He is the one who created you, and He sees you as special and valuable. Because of that, knowing Him in a personal way is our only hope in this life."

"Can I keep this poem?" she asked. "I want to read it again."

I smiled. "I thought you might. That's why I printed this copy for you. We can talk about it more after you read it a few more times. Okay?"

"Yeah. Sounds good. Thanks, Holly. You know, I feel better already. Like maybe God wants to write another poem with my life; I just don't know what it is yet."

"I think you're right, Angela. A new poem will be written. And I can't wait to read it."

The Losing Battle

The battle for Angela's soul was evident. What I hadn't known was the physical battle going on behind the scenes. Angela secretly had an eating disorder. Daily, she'd discreetly go into her bathroom and purge all of the food from her body.

Her suitemates eventually heard her throwing up. When they asked if she was sick, she claimed she was feeling fine. Over the course of the following weeks, her suitemates heard the sounds of purging more and more often. Finally, one day, they knocked and opened her door. Angela was lying weak and sickly in her bed. They pleaded with her to tell them what was going on.

Not wanting to give an answer, Angela asked them to just leave her alone so she could rest. With great concern, they came to my door and told me Angela was very sick. They said she'd been throwing up constantly for the past two weeks but seemed to be hiding it.

Immediately, I went to Angela's room and rushed to her bed. Sitting down next to her on her bed, I held her hand and asked her what was wrong.

She quickly shook her head and said, "I'm fine." Then she looked away.

"Angela, clearly you're not fine. Your eyes are bloodshot and your face doesn't seem its normal color. What's causing you to throw up? Your suitemates said you've been throwing up a lot recently. Are you sick? Pregnant?"

She shook her head but remained silent, still looking away.

"Angela, you don't have to open up to me if you don't want to, but I care, and I am here for you. Remember that poem I gave you? It says that God knows all your ways, and He is with you. Maybe there is something you aren't ready to share with me that you can talk to God about, since He already knows what is going on and cares for you."

Angela finally turned to look at me and stated, "I'm bulimic. It's the only way I know to stay thin and keep my image. I've been purging since I was 12 years old. I don't even know if it's possible to stop."

"Oh, Angela." Once again I was at a loss for words. I am not a trained counselor, and I didn't know what would help her out of this pattern. I asked the Holy Spirit to give me wisdom.

I said, "Angela, do you want to stop? If there was a way, would you want to know about it?"

"I don't know. How would I stay thin?"

"What if there was a way to stop purging and learn how to keep your body healthy? Would you want to learn how to do that?"

"Maybe . . ."

"Okay. Well, let me look into some options and I'll get back to you."

The Ranch

It had been almost a week, and Angela hadn't been able to attend any classes. Her body was just too drained. She seemed to be withering away. I learned that there was a ranch about an hour away that housed and counseled women with eating disorders. I asked Angela if she'd be interested in checking it out.

She nodded.

We went together that weekend to check it out. The property was spacious and nicely manicured, and the staff seemed very personable. We spotted a chapel and went inside. A sign displayed daily service times for girls who wanted to attend.

Angela liked that the ranch provided resources for her to learn proper nutrition and healthy exercise routines, and one-on-one counseling sessions; but she was most excited about the opportunity to attend chapel every day. She wanted to learn more about this God who loved her. Within the hour, Angela decided this was the place for her, and she decided to move in the next day.

Two weeks later, I went to visit her. As I entered her bedroom, which she shared with another girl, she proudly showed me her wall. Next to her bed was prominently displayed the handwritten copy of Psalm 139 that I had given to her. With a big smile, she said, "I've memorized the whole thing! I've been going to chapel every day, and I love the words we sing about God. I never knew He loved me so much! I love being here. They have us on a strict schedule, with high accountability, but slowly I can see that I'm having fewer urges to purge. Thank you for bringing me to this place! You saved my life!"

I remember driving the hour ride back to campus thanking God for saving her life. I remember praying for her to grasp the gospel so that both her soul and her body could become whole again.

The rest of that semester, Angela and I wrote letters back and forth. During the summer, Angela was released from the program. I didn't know it until one of my letters to her was returned to me. I called the ranch, but they weren't allowed to give me her personal information. Disappointed, because I, too, had changed addresses, all I could do was pray for her to someday, somehow, find another way to contact me.

Twelve years later, she found me—on Facebook.

The Facebook Message

I was at a conference when I got the invitation on Facebook to become "friends" with Angela. I couldn't believe it! I quickly accepted it and started looking at her page. I couldn't wait to write her a message when I got home to find out what had happened in her life over the past decade.

Unfortunately, I never got the chance to follow up with her. The very next day her boyfriend, Mark, messaged all of her friends on her Facebook account, sharing that Angela had tragically died the night before. Tears streamed down my face as I sat in the conference room reading this news on my cell phone. Then I continued to read the message.

Mark wrote that he was doing all of the funeral arrangements because Angela had no family that was willing to organize her service and burial. He said that because she had converted from Islam to Christianity, her dad had disowned her years ago, treating her as if she were already dead.

I couldn't believe it! After all of these years not knowing what happened to Angela, I learned that she had at some point decided to follow Jesus! I wrote back to Mark, asking for more of her story, but I soon realized he didn't know much of her background. In fact, he messaged me, asking if I could share more about the faith Angela had. He said it was apparent that her faith brought her hope, healing and joy despite the difficult journey she had lived.

While she and Mark were dating, he hadn't really wanted to ask more questions about her faith; but in her death, he couldn't help but long for the same hope, healing and joy she had found. I asked if we could talk on the phone, and he agreed.

Once again, with tears in my eyes, I asked the Spirit to give me wisdom to talk to this stranger who was hurting and seeking. What could I say to him in such a deep time of grief?

Poem of Hope and Healing

Our phone conversation was a little awkward at first as I tried to talk to a stranger about some deep issues. I didn't know what to say. I empathized with the heavy loss he'd just experienced two days ago, but I had no clue how I could enter into his pain. In grief counseling, I had been taught that a good first step is to talk about the person who has just passed away. I began by asking him to tell me about Angela. What did she do for work? How did they meet? What did he enjoy about her? What would he miss the most?

Though some of these questions were very personal, Mark shared openly because he knew she and I had been close friends in the past. He knew that I had the same faith Angela had, and he wanted to better understand it. Both of us were emotional on the phone. I kept praying that the Holy Spirit would show me how to comfort him.

As I listened to Mark and the Holy Spirit, it became clear that I was to share the same poem I had shared with Angela over a decade ago—the one she had cherished and memorized and that had ultimately changed her view of how God saw her. I pulled out my Bible and asked Mark if I could read to him Psalm 139. He said sure. With a shaky voice and tears flooding my eyes, I began to read it out loud.

At certain verses, I felt led to stop and emphasize particular points. "God knew her, Mark. God loved her. God created her. God had every day planned for her. And God knows you. God loves you. God created you. And God has a plan for you, as well, if you're willing to ask Him what it is. He can enter into your grief and bring you comfort when no one else is with you."

"How?" he asked. "How do I take this poem and make it real in my life?"

"Well, that's where God's loving Son, Jesus, comes into the picture. God loved us so much, yet He knew we were independent, prideful people. Our pride and independence are what keeps us separated from God, who knows and loves us. We cannot experience all He wants to do in and through our lives unless we have a personal relationship with Him. That is why Jesus came to earth. Someone who had a perfect relationship with God needed to die to take away our sin of independence and pride. When we put our faith in Jesus, we can have a relationship with God the Father. Only then can we experience God and live the life He wants us to live. Would this step of believing in Jesus be something you'd like to do today?"

"I don't know. It's a lot to take in right after Angela's passing."

"That's okay. I understand. Well, for now, maybe you can take comfort in this poem as Angela did. If you have any further questions about how to begin a relationship with Jesus, you can always call or Facebook me. How does that sound?"

"Yeah, that sounds good. Thanks for taking time to talk to a complete stranger. I see you have the same hope and joy that Angela had, even through your tears. Thanks for caring for her when she was younger, and thanks for caring for me now. Please keep praying for me when you think of it."

"You're welcome. And of course I will keep praying for you, Mark."

I never heard from Mark again, but I knew the message of God's love and comfort had been given to him. It was now up to Mark to choose to receive it.

MOMENT OF REFLECTION

Search me, O God, and know my heart! Try me and know my thoughts! And see if there be any grievous way in me, and lead me in the way everlasting!
PSALM 139:23-24

I have shared the gospel with many people throughout the years. Even if they appreciated the dialogue, few made a decision in the moment. At first, that greatly discouraged me. I wanted to see the gospel "work." My expectation changed when God displayed to me His plan of continually working in Angela's life after she left my dorm in college. I now know without a doubt that the gospel does work. It simmers in people's hearts and minds. Once the Word gets planted, it doesn't come back void. Still, it is each person's choice to accept it or reject it. I am not responsible for the decision. I am just the messenger.

The beauty of being a messenger who is filled with the Spirit is that we get to enter into the depth of someone's pain and bring him or her to the healing hand of Jesus. He or she may not grab it right away, but even knowing it is an option can often begin to bring comfort.

- *We don't need to be intimidated by someone's spiritual background.*
When I first heard that Angela was Muslim, I didn't feel equipped
to talk with her, but the Spirit showed me that He could guide
me in a conversation, even if I did not fully understand her spiritual background. No other religion has the power that the
gospel has, so we have no reason to feel intimidated by other religions (see Rom. 1:16).

- *We might be the only family, or community, a person has.* As our society becomes more individualistic, fewer people have close connections with others. We should not assume that a person has a
best friend or has other people to hang out with on weekends.
We truly might be the first person to befriend someone in a
meaningful way (see Col. 4:5-6).

- *Sometimes people need outside help—someone other than us—and that's
okay, even good.* The Holy Spirit will guide us as we seek Him in
conversations, and He will give us wisdom that is of God, but we
should not assume that we (in and of ourselves) have all the wisdom that one person needs. We need to be willing to advise people to see those (pastors and counselors) who have been trained
to help in areas we have not been trained in (see Eph. 4:7,11).

- *We may never know on this side of heaven if the seeds we planted took
root, but sometimes we get a glimpse.* And it makes it all worth it.
Don't be discouraged if you see yourself "just" planting. It's not
the end of that person's story, or yours (see 1 Cor. 3:6).

Holly A. Melton

Questions to Ponder

1. Are there certain spiritual backgrounds that intimidate you more than others? Why do you think that is so?

2. How might you bring the lonely into your family or community or church?

3. Is there anyone you know who has an addiction that needs outside help? How can you be a part of walking through that process with them?

Conversation with God

1. Ask the Holy Spirit to help you to not be intimidated by other spiritual backgrounds.

2. Ask the Holy Spirit to give you eyes to see who has no community and who needs a friend.

3. Ask the Holy Spirit to give you wisdom to know how to enter into someone's pain (loss of a family member, abuse, loss of a job, infertility, a wayward child, addictions) and how to know when you should encourage him or her to talk to someone else.

4. Keep praying for those you've shared the gospel with but who have not yet made the decision to put their faith in Jesus for salvation.

Chapter 4

Meeting Picasso

We are not all called to go to the mission field overseas, but we are all called to play a role in global missions. One role is to send missionaries overseas by supporting them financially. Another role is to pray for people in countries where few have heard the gospel. God wants to connect our hearts to people, even people we don't know, through prayer. We often think about prayer as connecting us to God, yet prayer can also be a powerful way to connect our hearts to people and their hearts to God. I became convinced that prayer connects us to people when I started praying for Picasso.

Prayer Commitment

Picasso was the code name of an art student living in East Asia. The only reason I started praying for Picasso was because my friend Shane asked me to. After graduating from university, Shane felt called to go overseas to a closed country in East Asia to share the gospel with college students. He was the first missionary I committed to partner with in prayer and finances, and I wanted to take my commitment seriously.

Shane met Picasso on campus, and they started meeting weekly to talk about spiritual things. Picasso seemed to be hungry to learn about God and the Bible, but having been raised in a country that says there is no God, it was hard for him to make the decision to follow Jesus.

I had no emotional or relational connection to Picasso. I hadn't even seen a picture of him because it could potentially jeopardize his safety if the government found out that he was attending Bible meetings. I started to pray for him for two reasons: First, Shane was my friend, and I wanted to pray for whatever he asked me to pray for. Second, I wanted to grow in praying for people who weren't in my direct sphere of influence.

I didn't know what to pray, but I knew that the Bible says the Holy Spirit can intercede for us on things we don't know much about (see Rom. 8:26). My meager attempts to pray for Picasso began like this: "Jesus, make yourself real to Picasso. You know his real name. You know where he is in this world. Show him the truth of the gospel. Give him the courage to accept You in a place where it is illegal to do so." I didn't know what else to pray, so I continued to ask the Holy Spirit to show me and to pray with me.

As I continued to persevere in praying for Picasso, I began to get more excited to pray for him, because new ideas would come to me as I read the Bible or thought about what life would be like in a closed country.

"God, have Picasso meet other believers that are his nationality . . ."

"God, have Picasso hunger to read Your Word . . ."

"God, give him courage to say yes to You, even though it means he will suffer for his faith."

"God, reveal yourself to him in a dream."

"God, raise him up to be a spiritual leader in this nation with few male leaders."

It might sound funny, but I started to think about Picasso more often and pray for him at times outside of my scheduled prayer time. I started to feel like we were friends, even though I had never interacted with him.

Prayer Connection

About nine months into this prayer journey, I received an email from Shane, telling me that Picasso had decided to put his faith in Jesus.

I was so elated that I jumped up and ran to tell my roommate what had happened. Tears of joy flooded my eyes as I thanked God for answering my prayers for a person I had never met, on the other side of the world. It was the first time I felt emotionally connected to a person with whom I wasn't necessarily friends. I was convinced that prayer connected me to him and prayer connected him to Jesus.

Over the course of the following year, Shane kept me updated on Picasso's growth as a new believer and how he was beginning to disciple others in their secret underground meetings held weekly in Shane's home. He asked me to pray that Picasso would be a witness to others, that he would stay strong in his faith, and that he'd truly grow to be a spiritual leader. I was committed more than ever to pray for this man. I knew God had a purpose for his life, and I wanted to be a part of it.

Near the end of Shane's two years of ministering in East Asia, I was asked to bring my own missions team into Shane's city for the summer. I was so excited to go visit my friend, but I was even more eager about possibly meeting my new brother-in-Christ, Picasso. To my great disappointment, Shane informed me that it would be very unlikely for me to meet Picasso. It wasn't safe for foreigners to interact with nationals or for us to meet students they had built relationships with.

I almost cried when I heard that! To be in the same city as Picasso but not get to meet him after praying for him for almost two years just seemed incredibly unfortunate, but I had to trust God and my friend Shane. I knew God could make a way if He wanted us to meet. It felt like a long shot, but I prayed that in a city of more than five million people, I'd run into Picasso.

Entering a Foreign Land

Even though Shane had gone before me, landing in this "closed" country for the first time was a huge step of faith for me. To lead a team of students to a place I'd never been before required me to daily listen to the wisdom and voice of the Holy Spirit.

We were not allowed to say words like "Jesus," "God," "Christian," "Bible," "church" or any other word that might trigger the attention of the people around us. We didn't know if our apartment or phones were bugged, so we used code words, even in our homes. We couldn't sing worship songs, and we couldn't pray with our eyes closed in public. We locked our Bibles in a safe every time we left home.

It was a totally new environment in which we had to trust God for our protection, but also for wisdom on how we would engage in spiritual conversations with students we met every day on campus.

We were advised not to get into a spiritual conversation the first time we met with someone, because they might be searching for missionaries undercover. Only after meeting with someone a few times could we start to engage in spiritual conversations. If the students seemed interested in talking about spiritual things, we were to try to meet with them off campus to share the gospel.

Daily, we prayed for the Holy Spirit to bring us to the right people to talk with. We'd often use lunchtime to sit down beside students in the cafeteria and strike up a conversation. Most of them were more than willing to talk, even offering to buy us our lunch so that they could practice and improve their English skills. Few had ever met an American, and they were full of questions of what life was like in the West, a place they associated with freedom and prosperity.

The Cafeteria Conversation

On one particular day, the school cafeteria was especially crowded. I joined a girl who was sitting alone at the edge of a long, steel table. She hadn't been very interested in conversing, so I slowed down my inquisitive talk and focused more on picking up the eggplant, chicken and rice with my wooden chopsticks. As soon as she got up to leave, a strapping young man swooped in to sit in her place. His smile and energetic movements made him appear as if he thought he was meeting someone famous by getting the seat across from me.

As he began to chat with me, I was impressed by his incredibly good English and enticed by his charming personality.

"Well, hello! I can't believe I get to sit here for lunch! Where are you from?"

"The United States." I still wasn't sure if I was to be stoic or to smile, so I stayed reserved.

"Wonderful! What state?"

"California." Okay, he was cute. I was starting to get excited about my new lunch mate.

"Oh, I've heard a lot about California. I have friends here who are from there. I hope I can visit there someday. It seems like paradise. What are you doing here in this city?"

"Studying the language."

"Nice! Want to speak it with me?"

"Ha, ha! No, thanks! Your English is much better!"

"Do you know any other foreigners here?"

"I've met some."

His questions came so fast that I started to feel uncomfortable. Maybe he wasn't being genuine, and he was an undercover government official that I had been warned about. Maybe he wanted to see if I was here for other intentions besides schooling.

I was appreciative of the training we'd received before we came here on how to deflect certain questions so as to not be too specific with our answers. But then, as if he was on to me, he asked more directly, "Do you know Shane?"

My eyes popped open in surprise when I heard my friend's name, but I cautiously tried to evade the question and focus more on him.

"I don't know. I've met quite a few foreigners since I've been here. I don't remember all of their names. What's your name, by the way? Here we are talking, and we haven't even introduced ourselves. My name is Holly, what's yours?"

He shared a name I could not pronounce. I just smiled, nodded and asked him, "So, what are you studying here at university?"

"Art History. I love to paint and I love to learn about the different styles of art from various time periods. It is one way for me to learn about the world outside the walls of this country."

I had never thought about that. There is so much I take for granted as a result of growing up in a country that values freedom.

Holly A. Melton

Before I could ask another question, this overly excited gentleman started sharing with me how two years ago he had met another foreigner from California, named Shane. Instantly, I felt lightheaded as my mind started to spin. My eyes opened wider as I listened to him. Could it be? Was I sitting in front of Picasso? He was an art major. I tried to remember to breathe as I listened to him talk.

"Shane and I became friends as we hung out weekly and started talking about the deeper meaning of life. We discussed the spiritual side of life, which I was intrigued with, having seen many paintings in my art history classes from cathedrals all over the world. Stories I did not know. Artists who had a passion to paint about a God I had never heard of.

"Then one day Shane shared with me a little yellow booklet called *The Four Spiritual Laws*." He pulled out the same booklet from his front pocket and, looking up at me earnestly, asked, "Have you ever seen this booklet before?"

I almost laughed out loud at his innocent but ironic question. This was the same booklet and question we were trained to use whenever we shared the gospel with someone! Could it be that Picasso was witnessing to me? Here was a believer, in a closed country, approaching a foreigner, in a public cafeteria as he pulled out the little yellow booklet to share the gospel!

Divine Interaction

I couldn't stop my jaw from dropping or a tear from escaping my eye. God had answered my prayer to meet Picasso, and here he was, sitting right in front of me.

Without answering his question, I said, "Wait. Let's backtrack. I do know Shane. We were friends back in California. Actually, I think he might have told me about you in some of his emails. He asked me to start praying for you two years ago when he met you, but he never told me your real name. He just called you Picasso because you were an art major. I've been praying for you consistently ever since. I never thought I'd get to meet you, but here you are sitting in front of me!"

Picasso's eyes also filled with tears as he started to comprehend what I was saying. Almost overcome with emotion, he said, "I just knew God wanted me to sit with you, but I didn't know why. I thought He wanted me to share my story and the gospel with you. But it seems like He wanted me to meet my prayer angel. I didn't know anyone was praying for me and my salvation. This means that we are family! You're my sister!" As that realization hit, Picasso jumped out of his seat, grabbed me by the arm and smothered me in a hug in the middle of the cafeteria. It was as if I had found my lost brother, and nothing else in the world mattered.

We sat back down, still full of wonder and joy, and I felt a bond like I had never felt before. We both knew this was a divine meeting, and we sat for a few moments in sweet silence, just smiling, laughing and looking into each other's eyes in amazement. Then, as if we'd been friends forever, Picasso started to share with me all that had happened to him since he decided to follow Jesus a little over a year ago.

Following Jesus = Persecution

"When Shane shared the gospel with me, I knew it was true, but it took time for me to really grasp it. I prayed to receive Jesus into my life on a park bench with the smells of spring and new life in the air. Shane encouraged me to immediately share my decision to follow Jesus with my roommates, but he warned me that they might not be as responsive to the gospel as I was.

"I went back to the dorms excited but, looking back, also a bit naive. I had three roommates at the time. When I came into the room and showed them the little yellow booklet that explained there is a God that loves us and wants to have a personal relationship with us, they started to laugh, called me a fool and told me I had lost my mind. I tried to disagree with them and started to read the booklet out loud, hoping they would hear the truth of the words. One of the guys got up from his stool and punched me in the face to get me to stop reading. I fell to the ground, hurt and shocked. I hadn't expected this new discovery of God to be received with such anger and hostility.

"The day after I was hit in the face, one of my other roommates asked if I still believed in God. I said 'Yes. I believe He is the way, the truth and the life. I cannot deny what is true.' Without a word he stood up, walked over to me, looked into my eyes with a mixture of pity and anger and then spat in my face.

"The following week, I was called out of one of my art classes and asked to go to the administration office. There, I was interrogated and asked if I was now a Christian, openly sharing my new beliefs with other students. I was warned that if another student complained about my openness of faith, I would be kicked out of university, never to return.

"I'm here on scholarship. It's my senior year. But I'm willing to lose it all if that's what God wants. I still meet with students and share the gospel with them. We have an underground ministry where we study the Bible and learn how to become more like Jesus. It hasn't been an easy road, but it's been worth it. Thank you for praying for me. My life could have looked very different without the prayers of believers like you."

As I listened to his journey, I realized he had experienced more trials and persecution in his first year of being a believer than I had my entire life! It humbled me that I had the opportunity to meet him and the privilege to continue to pray for his life's impact in his country.

The Party

Three weeks after I met Picasso, it was time for our team to head back home. Our last night in the country, we had a good-bye party. We invited the new friends we had made over the course of six weeks. Many of them had put their faith in Christ or were interested in dialoguing further about spiritual things. We wanted to have this party so that they could connect with each other, as well as with other Asian believers.

Picasso was invited to the party too. He had brought his cousin along, who was also a believer in Jesus. After Picasso introduced us, she clung by my side for most of the party. At one point in the evening, she looked at me contemplatively and asked, "Have you fallen in love with the people in this country?" It seemed like such an odd yet innocent question. But as soon as she asked it, I knew what the answer was, "Yes. I guess I have!"

"That's what I thought!" she said. "I can tell by the way you speak with the students that a little bit of your heart is going to stay here when you leave tomorrow. I know this may seem out of the blue, but would you pray and consider coming back for a longer amount of time? It seems to me that it's easier for college students here to listen to foreigners talk about Jesus than to hear it from their own people. At least that seemed to be true in my cousin's case. Look at how many students are here tonight that decided to believe in Jesus in just the past six weeks! What could happen if you came back for a year and brought more people with you?"

This woman had no idea that I was a part of a ministry back home and that I actually had the ability to come back if I wanted to. All she knew was that I loved Jesus and had prayed for her cousin. She also saw how being in this country and sharing Christ had impacted my heart.

The Flight Home

Her question was all I could think about when I tried to sleep that final night in East Asia. As our plane lifted off the next morning, I could see the country expanding below me. Tearfully, I started to pray and ask the Holy Spirit if He wanted me to come back.

My mind started to list all the changes I would need to adapt to if I chose to go live there: I'd have to leave the comforts of a first-world country; I'd have to use squatty potties; I'd have to live in dense smog, which required many people to wear masks over their mouths to breathe; I'd have to learn the language well enough to use public transportation and buy food; and I'd have to get used to the reality of people stopping to point at me and stare because I'd be one of the few Caucasian people in a city of five million.

None of those changes or challenges compared to the joy of seeing lives changed with prayer and the power of the gospel.

As I thought back over the past two years of praying for Shane and Picasso, it was clear to me that prayer connects us to others. Prayer had connected me to Picasso, and Picasso had connected my heart to the people in his country. As his cousin pointed out, this country was hungry for the gospel. Shane's team was heading home in a few months, and another team needed to be raised up to take their place. It seemed like God was saying that it was my turn now; I just had to follow His lead. Before the plane landed in California, I had peace that the Holy Spirit wanted me to return.

MOMENT OF REFLECTION

Continue steadfastly in prayer,
being watchful in it with thanksgiving.
COLOSSIANS 4:2

My choice to pray for a missionary and enter into his world changed my view of prayer forever. The Holy Spirit wants us to pray for lost people, even people far, far away. He wants to connect our hearts with people we haven't met before. Maybe it happens with a child you choose to support through Compassion International or some other agency; maybe it's a pastor you learn about who lives in a Muslim country and is undergoing persecution for his faith; or maybe it's a young missionary going overseas for the first time.

As we choose to enter in and pray for people, our hearts become intertwined with them in a real way. This is true partnership in prayer. It is not just for people who say they have the gift of prayer, but it is also for anyone who asks the Holy Spirit to show him or her how to pray.

- *The Holy Spirit can connect our hearts to others all over the world.* As we pray for missionaries and the people they interact with, we are truly partnering with them in the gospel (see Eph. 6:18-20).

- *The Holy Spirit will show us what to pray as we continue to ask Him what to pray for* (see Rom. 8:26).

- *The Holy Spirit connects our prayers to the person in a way that is supernatural.* There may be moments when we will get a glimpse of how we are a part of what God is doing all over the world through our faithful prayers.

- *We are each called to be a part of the Great Commission—whether it's to pray, give financially, go ourselves or a mixture of all three.* As we listen to His leading, we will know what role to play (see Matt. 28:18-20).

- *You can lead others, even to places you haven't been to, if you listen to the guidance of the Holy Spirit* (see Deut. 31:6).

Questions to Ponder

1. Do you know of missionaries, or other people, you can pray for who are living in another country? If you don't, ask your church about any missionaries they support or have sent out, and begin praying for them. Ask to receive their prayer letters or ministry updates. Take time to read and pray over them.

2. What can help you increase your commitment to pray for others you don't know personally yet? Perhaps start by praying for a missionary with your small group or Sunday School class, or pray with your spouse. It's wonderful to see how the Holy Spirit can guide the prayer time in a small group of people for an individual you haven't met yet.

3. What might the Holy Spirit be asking you to do to be a part of the Great Commission in this stage of your life? (Pray? Give? Go?)

Conversation with God

1. Ask God to show you who to begin praying for and "adopting" into your prayer time.

2. Ask the Spirit to show you what to pray. Take time to listen for His leading.

3. Ask the Spirit if you are to give toward a certain need or cause. Ask Him to use your finances for His kingdom and to further the gospel, so as to store up treasures in heaven.

4. Ask the Spirit if you are to go and minister to a certain people or place. He doesn't call all people to be in vocational ministry or travel overseas to some foreign land, but we are all called to minister where we currently are—at home or abroad.

Chapter 5

The Death of
My Best Friend

I have traveled to more than 25 countries, asking people of different cultures, backgrounds and ages what they desire most in life. Whether they live in North Africa, the Middle East, East Asia, Europe or the United States, the answers are very similar. Some people dream about fame and fortune. Many more people express a desire for peace and freedom. But the answer I hear over and over again, stated in various ways, is that they want to be fully known and fully loved. They long for someone to know them intimately—to know their good and their bad—and still love them deeply.

How can it be that such a global desire seems to be a mystery to find? I believe it is because those who have found it and experienced it have not shared their story of being known and loved by God.

There are stories that just must be told. Throughout the ages, certain stories have been passed down from generation to generation. Even as times change, these stories continue to bring hope and joy to our lives. Our own personal stories should be stories that must be told, especially when we have found the source of unconditional love and acceptance. Sometimes we receive the greatest joy when we tell the stories that need to be told from our own lives.

I am convinced that presenting Jesus in the story of our lives can be attractive to any people group of any culture, at any time. I am not saying that every person, at any moment, wants to hear our story, but we need to believe that our stories about Jesus have supernatural power to impact the hearts of the people around us. We need to be willing to step out in faith; we need to be willing to ask the Holy Spirit to guide us and practice thinking outside the box when it comes to sharing the story of the gospel and the impact it's had on our lives.

Journey to the Far Side of the City

I lived for two years in a small, East Asian city of five million people. I visited college campuses all over the city to engage with college students. I had no clue how my story of faith could connect with students who have been taught by their government that there is no God. Where does one start the conversation when the person doesn't even know she can think about believing in a higher power than her government?

As my roommate Elsa and I left our apartment and journeyed on a bus to a campus on the far side of the city, we prayed for three things: for the Spirit to give us His wisdom what to say; for courage to step out in faith; and for Him to connect us to people whose hearts were open to hearing the gospel.

As our bus traveled to the outskirts of the city, the land became barren and desolate. Outside the high walls of the campus, we saw no homes, stores or restaurants. Thirty thousand students lived within those walls, with nowhere else to go and nothing else to do. This campus was opened only six years ago, but as we entered the gates to the campus, we saw that the new buildings were covered with dust from the continual construction.

It was around 2:00 PM, right after their nap time, and most students were heading to their classes. We walked around the dusty grounds, praying that we could find a student who would want to engage with us about their school, their life and, ultimately, the gospel.

As we walked against the flow of students leaving their dorm rooms for class, we felt like salmon swimming upstream. My mind started to flood with doubts: *Maybe we should come back another day? Maybe we should just prayer walk instead of looking for people to talk to.* But I pushed those thoughts to the side, and we pressed on. We asked the Holy Spirit, again, to show us some women we could talk to.

The Little Rock Garden

A few moments later, as we approached a little rock garden, Elsa and I noticed two girls talking at a stone table. We immediately altered our course and pushed through the crowded sidewalk of students to head toward them. As we reached their stone table, the young women looked up and their faces registered surprise. I was finally getting used to the stares and shocked first glances when these sheltered students saw my blonde hair and white skin. I smiled to break the ice and asked if we could join them to learn more about their life here on campus. They nodded their heads with eager smiles, and patted the table for us to join them.

"My name is Holly, and this is my friend Elsa. We are visiting your campus today to meet with students and learn what life is like out here for you. What are your names?"

"I'm Samantha, and this is my best friend Rachel." I assumed they had given me their English names assigned in their English class because I had initiated the conversation in English. I was thankful, because English names are easier for me to remember.

After asking questions about their focus of studies, their families and their values in life, I wasn't sure how to guide the conversation to spiritual things. I learned that they both came from the countryside and that Samantha came from a village steeped in Buddhism. I was praying silently for the Spirit to give me questions that would enable us to share the gospel, but at this point I wasn't sensing any clear direction or questions.

I figured I could just start with the basics, so I asked, "What do you like most about being in college?"

Rachel shrugged her shoulders and said, "Hanging out with our friends."

"What do you like to talk about most with your friends?"

They smiled at each other with chins turned down shyly and then looked up at me. With fluttering eyelashes, Samantha quietly whispered, "Love." Then they both covered their mouths and giggled in embarrassment.

I smiled, agreeing with them. It seemed like the topic of love came up in almost any conversation I had with students. Everyone seemed to desire the same thing—unconditional love.

Before I had the chance to think of another question, Samantha sighed and admitted, "I am too idealistic. I want a love I will never receive; yet I look for it, crave it, hope for it, even though part of me doubts it can ever be found."

I nodded at her, realizing that in a sense, she was exactly right. I said, "You know, Samantha, everyone everywhere desires that type of love. You're not alone, or silly, for wanting that type of love in a relationship. We were all created for that. It is okay to want that love. It's natural."

A Friend Like No Other

In that moment, I knew the Holy Spirit wanted me to share with these two girls the gospel in story form. I had never done that before. I had no clue what that would sound like, so I asked the Spirit to give me wisdom, and He opened my mouth.

"I had a best friend," I began. "This friend knew me better than anyone. He knew my secrets, my weaknesses, my failures; and yet he pursued me and said he loved me perfectly. Even when I was unfaithful to him, he loved me. He forgave me.

"What do you believe is the greatest way someone could display his or her love to you?" I asked.

Samantha replied, "When people encourage me with words and want to spend time with me."

Rachel replied, "When people tolerate my faults, like my parents do."

Then Samantha tilted her head and asked, "What would perfect love look like to you?"

I said, "Well, this friend, he loved me perfectly. You see, I did a lot of bad things. Very unloving things toward other people, and I was going to be brutally punished. But you know what my friend said to me? 'I will take the punishment for you.' I was perplexed because he had done nothing wrong, yet he quietly took my beating for me. Grievously, the punishment was so severe that he didn't survive. My friend died that day. It should have been me. But he died instead."

They looked at me questioningly, wondering if they had heard me correctly in their second language. With a nod, I repeated, "He died."

They looked at Elsa to translate because they still couldn't comprehend. As Elsa reiterated what I'd said in their native language, their eyes instantly filled with shock and tears. It appeared that both were amazed that someone would take on my punishment to the point of death.

Meeting My Best Friend

I cleared my throat and continued. "The miraculous thing is that even though I cannot physically see him, he feels closer to me than any other person. He still guides me, comforts me, and loves me more deeply than anyone. There is only one condition in our relationship. I can never think that our closeness is because of anything I do. We are friends because of his choice to pursue me and love me perfectly. What's amazing is how I have changed because of his sacrificial love. I am able to love others much more fully and deeply. I've also noticed that I have greater peace, joy and purpose in my life. He is such an amazing friend. It brings me great joy to share with others about him so that they, too, can experience his love for them and have a joy-filled and purposeful life. Would you want to meet him?"

Both Samantha and Rachel nodded, not even questioning how they could meet someone who had died. Hope filled their eyes, and they listened as I continued to tell the story that the Spirit had laid on my heart.

"My friend's name is Jesus."

They recognized His name, but I continued on, emphasizing how I related to Him personally. "He isn't just a historical person. He is present with me now. Not because I've made Him up in my mind, but because He is actually alive today. Three days after He was killed, He rose from the dead and then ascended into heaven. Though He is not physically on earth, His Spirit is very close to me. I have never seen His face or touched Him, yet He is very real and present in my life."

Rachel looked at her watch and saw that it was nearing the time for them to head to class. It was obvious they didn't want to leave. We knew our time was running short, so Elsa took over the conversation. In their own language she asked if they would like to know this Jesus more personally, like we do. They both said yes, and they would like their roommates to come and listen next time.

The Joy of His Friendship

As they were standing up to leave, Samantha smiled and said, "I am so excited to share this story of love and friendship with all of our roommates! I cannot believe someone could love us that much! To die for us! I am excited to meet with you again and learn more about Jesus. He is what I've been longing for, and I didn't even know it."

With huge smiles and tears blurring our sight, we hugged Samantha and Rachel and watched them walk away. Elsa and I sat back down on the stone benches, speechless. Our hearts were filled with peace and joy that reached the deepest crevices of our souls. Though the girls hadn't heard a four-point outline of the gospel, they heard the story of love, redemption and forgiveness. Their eyes cried out with hope that just maybe they, too, could receive that type of love.

When we could finally speak, we praised our precious Jesus in heaven as our hearts swelled with a new love and appreciation for our relationship with Him. In tears, we prayed for the salvation of those girls and the hearts of the 30,000 students on that campus. We were in awe, again, of how He allows us the privilege to share this amazing story of love and grace with others.

The Power of Our Story

Oh, the power of our story—of all Christians' story! To experience the power of our story as it reaches into strangers' hearts, giving them the hope that they can be pursued even though they have failed and been unfaithful! It is a story that enables them to feel for the first time that they are fully known and perfectly loved.

If we have a relationship with Jesus, then we have that love. The question is: Are we willing to share that love story with others? The greatest joy in the world can come through sharing the story that needs to be told—the story of love, the story of sacrifice, the story of Jesus.

MOMENT OF REFLECTION

Because our gospel came to you not only in word, but also in power and in the Holy Spirit and with full conviction.
1 THESSALONIANS 1:5

As I reflect back on that day in the garden, I am extremely humbled that God's purpose for us was to show His power through us so that His name might be proclaimed in all the earth.

One of the most beautiful things is to see someone grasp the story of the gospel for the first time. It brings the gospel to life for you, increasing your joy, faith and relationship with Him. Even when you still don't fully grasp the gospel, you become amazed by how the Holy Spirit opens the ears and hearts of people who have never heard the story before. This story of Jesus—our Savior,

Redeemer and Friend—must be told. It is too good to keep to ourselves. It must be, it will be, passed down from generation to generation, because it's not just a story; it's real. *He* is real.

As I walked through the conversation with Samantha and Rachel, these are the truths I discovered:

- *The Holy Spirit wants to show us how to share the story of Jesus over and over again, each time in a new, refreshing and impactful way to those who are listening.* We just need to ask Him to show us how (see Luke 11:9-13).

- *As we share the story with others, the Holy Spirit will include us on the journey of grasping once again the power and beauty of the gospel in our own lives.* Often, we will leave the conversation feeling closer to Him and incredibly grateful. The more we talk about our relationship with Him, the fonder our hearts will grow toward Him (see 1 Thess. 1:5-7).

- *As we come across obstacles in conversation and start to question whether we can lead the conversation to the topic of Jesus, we can ask the Holy Spirit to give us the questions to ask and the words to transition to the gospel.* The Holy Spirit does not want to hide the story of Jesus from others. If we ask Him to fill us and give us wisdom, He will show us clearly if the person is not interested, or He will give us a way to share the story with others. We must trust the voice of the Spirit as He guides us, and take the step of faith to ask what He puts on our mind to ask (see 1 John 2:20,27).

Questions to Ponder

1. What do you think is the most common longing people feel when they ponder their life? Do you agree that it is to be intimately known and perfectly loved? If so, how can you use this common desire to bridge into a conversation with others?

2. When was the last time you reflected on the story of the gospel? This is crucial if you want to communicate the gospel out of a heart of gratitude, rather than duty. The more we grasp the depth of the gospel's message, the more we'll take time to thank Jesus for what He's truly done for us, and the more confident we will become in communicating His story with others.

3. What doubts come to your mind when you are in a spiritual conversation with someone? What Scripture can you use to overcome those doubts? How can you battle those doubts while you are having the conversation?

Conversation with God

1. Ask the Holy Spirit to give you courage to press on through your fears and doubts and fill you with faith to engage with others.

2. Ask the Holy Spirit to open your eyes to the beauty and depth of the gospel.

3. Ask Him to show His power through you so that His name would be glorified.

4. Ask the Holy Spirit to lead you to people He is already pursuing. It is the Holy Spirit who pursues you before you become a follower of Jesus. It is the Holy Spirit who opens your eyes to your sin and the truth of the gospel. It is the Holy Spirit who seals you when you decide to put your faith in Jesus. He will lead you to someone He is already pursuing. Just ask.

Chapter 6

Boy Bands and Glow Sticks

There are moments in our lives when we feel stuck, not knowing what to do next. We've tried our own strategies and ideas, and things don't seem to be moving forward the way we envisioned. We start to feel hopeless when we can't picture the situation changing. At times, we choose to give up and walk away. Sadly, some of our passions, some of our dreams, die in the process.

This is especially true when we think about things that are way bigger than us, like governments, laws and policies we feel powerless to influence. We think about people we long for to come to Jesus, but they just seem so far from God.

I remember seeing a Nike sign on a brick wall in East Asia that said, "Impossible Is Nothing." Though bad English, the quote reminded me of the verse "For nothing will be impossible with God" (Luke 1:37). This is not just a flippant bumper sticker; it is God's Word. Do we really believe *nothing* is impossible with God? If we did, how would we pray differently? What would we step out in faith to try to do?

The Rule

I started to believe that nothing is impossible with God when I chose to head back to East Asia as a missionary. I saw glimpses of how plentiful the harvest was when I was there on a six-week missions trip a few years back. It seemed like once we shared the gospel with students, many of them put their faith in Jesus, even if it meant persecution. Like my friend Picasso did.

The fact that there were as many college students in this country as there were *people* in the United States made me wonder how we could ever reach them all with the gospel.

Those who had been serving long term in this country gave us "The Rule" that we needed to meet with students three times before we could share the gospel with them. This rule was put in place for our safety. Since we were in a closed country, it was illegal to share the gospel. We needed time with students to make sure they weren't members of the Communist party. If they were, they might be looking for foreigners like us who were not abiding by the rules of the land, and turn us in to the authorities. With this rule in place, however, it would take many more missionaries over many more years to spread the gospel to every student in East Asia.

After six months of following this rule, our team decided it was time to pray and fast and ask the Holy Spirit to give us a vision of what we could do to reach more students. We wanted to believe there was a way to go unnoticed by the government but still gather students into a group and share the gospel with them. If nothing is impossible with God, we wanted to see what idea He would give us to reach the thousands of college students in our city.

The Power of Prayer and Fasting

One week, as our team was studying passages on prayer and fasting, we were inspired when we read how many people in the Bible fasted and, as a result, saw the impossible become possible.

Nehemiah, for instance, heard that the walls of Jerusalem had been torn down and that the Jews were displaced, having no safe place to settle (see Neh. 1:4-11). He wept and mourned for days. He fasted and prayed to God on behalf of the sins of his people, and for God to give him favor before the king to whom he was a cupbearer.

One day, the king noticed Nehemiah's sadness of heart. No one was allowed to be sad around the king. It could have cost Nehemiah his life. When the king asked about his distress, Nehemiah said a quick prayer, probably under his breath, then stepped out in faith to ask the king's permission to go and rebuild the walls of Jerusalem. The king granted Nehemiah's request.

Though he had been given the king's permission to go, Nehemiah had no resources to do what God had placed on his heart to do. He stepped out in faith again and asked the king for a written letter that would allow him to pass through the land, sort of like a passport or visa. He also asked for timber to rebuild the wall. The king granted both requests.

Through prayer and fasting, Nehemiah was granted time off from his job and also given the resources to do the work. In just a little over 50 days, Nehemiah and the people rebuilt the walls of Jerusalem. God made the impossible possible.

Esther had a similar challenge when she heard there was a decree to destroy her people, the Jews. Even though she was now the queen, she had no authority to go talk to the king, even though he was her husband, unless he summoned her. If she approached him and he did not want to see her, she could be killed for being too forward. So, approaching the King to ask him to change a decree that he had already sealed with his signature seemed impossible.

Esther knew that she would need God's favor and protection if she were to go before the king, so she called a three-day fast for her and her people (see Esther 4:16). God gave her wisdom to approach the king and ask for the seemingly impossible request to save her people, the Jews, from annihilation. By the grace of God, Esther found favor with the king, and she and thousands of her people were saved.

Many others fasted in the Bible, including Moses, Daniel, King David and Jesus. Each fast had a different purpose, but the results were the same: God met with those who fasted, He heard their cries and made the impossible possible, for His glory.

When You Fast

Jesus said in Matthew 6:16, "When you fast," not *if* you fast. *When* we fast, we see God break strongholds, release resources, grant us favor with others, and we see the miraculous happen.

My first experience with fasting was when I was preparing to head to East Asia for a longer period of time. I wanted to hear from the Lord to receive clear vision for the mission ahead, and to know that I had His clear calling on my life. I prayed and fasted for 40 days. I didn't know it was even possible to fast for that long, but even fasting isn't impossible with God.

Reading the Word became my food. Those 40 days were the most intimate times with Jesus in my life. I was more sensitive to sin than I had ever been before. Even though I'm an extrovert, I longed for more time with the Lord rather than more time being with people. From my experience, I believe that we cannot be closer to the Lord on this side of heaven than when we are engaged in fasting and prayer.

Our Fast

We knew that our mission to reach every student in the city with the gospel was impossible unless we invited God into the situation. After studying about prayer and fasting, we decided as a team to pray and fast for a week. Some fasted by not eating food. Others needed food, so they fasted from things like watching TV or playing video games. The time we would usually spend eating or watching TV, we used to seek the Lord on our own.

Every night we gathered and sought Him together. We asked the Holy Spirit to increase our vision for this city. We asked Him to give us ideas on how to reach more students in a shorter amount of time, in a country where it is illegal to share the gospel. We asked the Lord to protect us from the government and to be able to fly under the radar. We asked Him to make the impossible possible.

In our own wisdom and brainstorming, we could not imagine how any of this could happen. It seemed like this country was ripe for revival, but how could we see it happen in such a restricted, oppressive environment?

During one of our prayer times, we were asking the Spirit to answer these particular questions: "What is something that college students enjoy that the rest of the faculty or government officials wouldn't care about? What would specifically attract college students to group together in this culture?"

As we prayed, the thought of music came to our minds. Students absolutely loved music. Boy bands were the craze, even among the guys. So we started to ask the Spirit, "What could we do with music?" The answer, though seemingly strange at first, was to create a boy band and hold a concert.

"But, Lord," we prayed, "how will we do that?"

Creation

The thought came to our mind to invite staff we knew from Singapore who had developed a band called "Creation." When we contacted them and asked if they'd be willing to put on a concert in our city, we learned that they had been praying for opportunities to do concerts in closed countries like ours! God was making the impossible possible, one prayer at a time, for both of us!

As we continued to pray about how to utilize the boy band, we got the idea of having three concerts. The first two would be held on opposite sides of the city, because our city was so populated and the campuses were geographically far apart. The third concert would be a follow-up concert for students who wanted to learn more about Jesus from what they'd heard during the first concert. We hoped that in this way we would get to share the gospel in a group setting with those who really wanted to hear it.

One huge blessing was having Hannah on our team. Hannah was Asian American and knew the language fluently, so she was able to go on her own to the three campuses to reserve the auditoriums for the concerts. If something went wrong at these concerts, or if authorities found out she was a foreigner, she could be deported and blacklisted from returning; but she was willing to take the risk. Although the rest of the team stayed behind to cover Hannah with prayer as she headed to the administration offices of three universities in our city, we hadn't really known how crucial praying would be.

Questioning

Hannah prayed on her walk to the first campus, asking the Holy Spirit to fill her with wisdom, courage and favor, just as Nehemiah had done before he approached the king to request letting him rebuild Jerusalem's walls. When Hannah entered the administration office, she handed the man behind the desk her room reservation request. He barely looked at her as he asked curtly, "What's this reservation for?"

Trying to conjure up a stoic expression, Hannah replied, "A gathering."

With suspicion in his eyes, he inquired, "Who are you?"

Staring straight ahead, and not wanting to give her name, she answered, "A student."

"Is this for a religious gathering?"

Hannah, praying under her breath, gave no reply.

He quickly continued, "It had better not be." Then he stamped the paper to approve the reservation for the auditorium that would hold 3,000 students, and handed it back to her.

As Hannah left the room, her hands were shaking. She praised God for keeping her mouth shut when needed and for giving her the right words to say to this man's questions. God had not just opened a door, but an entire auditorium that we could now use!

This situation vividly showed us how we each had unique roles to play in this outreach. We couldn't all do the same task or take the same step of faith. Hannah was able to take her step of faith because of her ethnicity and language ability. Part of being a team was praying and fasting together, and seeing what God wanted us to do as a group and as individuals.

The Concerts

The week before the first concert, we saturated the campuses with fliers and posters. We wanted every student to hear about it and have an opportunity to come. Though it was a public event, happening in a public place, we wanted only students to attend.

We couldn't prohibit others from coming, but we could make it less enticing by requiring anyone without a student ID to pay for a very expensive concert ticket. That worked! Though we had a place for people to buy tickets, not one ticket was purchased. Everyone who entered the doors for the concert had a student ID from one of the campuses in the area.

God knew how to work around the laws of the land, and it was getting us very excited to see what would happen next!

On opening night, the line outside the doors to the auditorium went down the stairs, along the sidewalk and curved around the building. People were waiting by the doors, anxious for them to open so that they could get good seats. The irony in the excitement was that Creation was an unknown band. None of the students attending this concert had heard of them, yet it was the biggest event the school had hosted in a long time. More than 2,600 students flooded into the auditorium that first night.

Sitting in the back with a black hoodie on in order to not draw attention to myself, I prayed for the students who were giggling and jumping around in anticipation. I prayed for the band as they entered the stage and started to play. The theme of the concert was "Journey of Love." The concert began with songs about falling in love, then progressed into songs about surviving a broken heart and closed with a song about our hearts longing for an eternal love.

Between songs, Joey, the lead singer, shared about his journey of love. He had been in a serious relationship with a girl he was certain was going to be his wife. She broke up with him to pursue another guy, turning his world upside-down. This led him into a deep depression that he didn't know how to get out of.

One day, he met a friend who shared about a love that is everlasting; he shared with Joey about the one who heals broken hearts and enables us to love again. Joey left his story as a cliffhanger. He invited the students to attend Creation's last concert at the end of the week. There, they would hear the rest of his story on how he found an everlasting love that changed his life forever.

The students each had glow sticks under their chairs. During the final song, about finding the love of his life, Joey invited the students to break the glow sticks to light up the auditorium if they, too, wanted to find this everlasting love. Stick after stick was broken and held high, glowing, as their hearts were stirred to find that love.

Though the gospel had not yet been presented, Joey's testimony moved the hearts of everyone in attendance. The room radiated with feelings of hope and anticipation as the students trickled outside, their glow sticks in hand, to head back to their respective campuses.

The following night, Creation played on the other side of the city. With fewer campuses, they still had an amazing turnout of more than 1,000 students in attendance. Again, hearts were stirred, tears were shed and glow sticks shined in the darkness as students heard the songs of a love that can never be lost. It felt like a holy moment. It was a secret sanctuary in the middle of a campus in a closed country, where the Spirit was most definitely moving. The impossible was becoming possible.

The Final Concert

We weren't sure what the turnout would be for the final concert after having almost 4,000 students attend the previous two concerts. This evening would go a little differently because we were going to clearly present the gospel. We needed God's protection like never before.

After much prayer and discussion, our team decided that because of the content of this concert, it would be too dangerous for those of us who were Caucasian to attend. We didn't want to draw attention to the event, nor have people think foreigners were hosting it. That left our teammate Hannah to oversee the evening without us.

Honestly, I was really discouraged that I wasn't able to attend. The first concert was so incredibly powerful, and I didn't want to miss out on whatever was going to happen that evening. As I

stayed home and prayed alongside my roommate, the Lord reminded me again that prayer is a powerful role to play. Hannah,
the students involved in our ministry, and the band needed our
prayers and the protection of God. After remembering this, we
were determined to take our role seriously, and we started praying. Prayer is what makes the impossible possible.

About half an hour into our prayer time, Hannah texted us
and said, "Please pray! The manager of the auditorium angrily approached us and said, 'If anything happens here tonight that I
don't approve of, I will pull the plug on the electricity and the
night will be over.' We cannot share the gospel if this man is in the
room. Please pray for God to protect us."

It seemed like another impossible situation! The man clearly
seemed to be looking out for any illegal activity to pounce on, like
a lion pounces on an innocent little lamb. My roommate and I
prayed that God would blind his eyes and mute his ears or give
him a stomachache so that he'd have to leave the room. The concert had begun and we didn't know what was going on until about
an hour later.

Hannah texted: "The manager's gone! He left right after the
first two songs and hasn't returned. Pray he stays away while the
gospel is shared." Another amazing answer to prayer! We learned
after the concert that the manager never came back into the room.
The auditorium was clearly protected by God. Only those He
wanted to hear were there.

As Joey shared how his relationship with Jesus brought him
out of depression into a life of hope, the room was blanketed in another holy silence. After he shared his story, linking it to a gospel
message, the band sang a song about Jesus' love for us on the cross.
On the screens behind the band, portions of "The Jesus Film" were
being shown so that the students could see with their own eyes
the story of His life, death and sacrifice. Eyes turned from the dis-
turbing scenes of Jesus being beaten and nailed to a cross. Weeping was heard around the room.

When the song was finished, the lead singer asked this question, "Do you want to open your heart to Jesus tonight and invite

Him into your life? If so, please pray this prayer to Him: 'Lord Jesus, I am a sinner. I know now that You love me so much that You died for me. You died for me so that I could be forgiven of my sin. I want to accept Your sacrifice on my behalf. Now I can have a personal relationship with the God who created me, knows me, and loves me. Please come into my life and make me the kind of person You want me to be. Show me how to follow You all the days of my life. Amen."

The room echoed as hundreds of students prayed this prayer out loud in their own language. Some were in the aisles, kneeling, crying and praying. Others were standing with their arms raised to the heavens, shouting the words—unashamed for the world to hear.

Questionnaires were passed out after the prayer. Students could mark if they made a decision to follow Jesus and if they'd like to meet with someone to learn more about this new relationship with Him. It was truly a night of praise and worship!

When Hannah came back to the house that evening, we stayed up to the wee hours of the morning, reading the cards. We were astounded and overjoyed to discover that 519 students had decided to follow Jesus that evening!

Here were some of their comments on the cards:

- "I experienced what love is tonight. If I have Jesus' love in my life, I can have real happiness in life."
- "I feel that tonight was not just a performance, but a heart-to-heart experience. I really, really want to know Jesus and learn more about Him. I love Him."
- "I really want to receive the Lord's love . . ."
- "You gave me courage to look for a new life."
- "Right now I especially need people's help. Tonight, I found it. I thank all of you. I think that after tonight I will have a better life."
- "I would like to know more about Jesus. If you have the opportunity, can you come to our school?"

Through our huge smiles and streaming tears, we praised God for His amazing work this week as we saw thousands of students

gather together in a Communist country and have the opportunity to hear and respond to the gospel.

Making Disciples

Jesus' commission to us, in Matthew 28:18-20, says to "Go therefore and make disciples . . ." not "Go and make converts." The
work was not over once the comment cards were collected and the
boy band left the city. Outreach was important, but trusting the
Holy Spirit to guide us as we followed up with these new believers
was just as vital.

During the next three weeks, we tried to meet face to face with
each of the 519 students who had indicated a decision to follow Jesus. What we weren't expecting was for them to bring their friends
to our follow-up meetings so that they could hear about Jesus too!
We spent most of our follow-up conversations sharing the gospel
and seeing even more students decide to follow Jesus! Revival was
exploding in the city, and more students were coming to Christ
than we had time to follow up!

To try to solve this challenge, we used the list of new believers
and started underground Bible studies on each campus. This was
a dangerous approach, because the government might catch on to
what we were doing, so we kept each study to no more than 10
people. Even with grouping the new believers together, there were
more than 70 groups, which was still too much for us to facilitate
on our own.

We asked the underground house church pastors if they would
help us, but because we didn't know the new believers personally,
we couldn't vouch that some weren't spies for the government. The
pastors apologetically said that they couldn't help us at the moment; but if, after a year, there were groups of students still meeting, they would gladly take them under their wing. Until then, it
was up to us, and the Holy Spirit, to figure out how to secretly disciple the 700-plus new believers. What a terrific problem to have!

When I had come to East Asia a few summers previously and
was asked by Picasso's cousin if I would come back, I had no clue

this would be the fruit of saying yes to go where the Spirit wanted me to go. *My* plan was to only be here for a year, but after seeing all of these new believers and realizing there were no systems in place to help disciple them, I knew the Spirit was leading me to stay at least another year. After that year, our team could transition the ministry to the local underground church communities.

Again, our team entered a time of prayer and fasting. We praised God for the changed lives and the revival happening under the nose of the government where it was illegal to gather together to study the Bible. We pleaded for His wisdom and direction as to how the 6 of us could follow up with 70 small groups. We did not have the time or capacity for each one of us to meet with 12 different groups each week. We needed the Lord to show us another way. That's when He brought to our attention the verses in 2 Timothy 2:1-2: "You then, my child, be strengthened by the grace that is in Christ Jesus, and what you have heard from me in the presence of many witnesses entrust to faithful men who will be able to teach others also."

My teammates and I felt like we were children, though all of us were in our 20s. The task before us seemed like something that older, wiser Christians should be handling. We clung to the encouragement in the verse to be strengthened by the grace that is in Christ Jesus. He would give us the wisdom to figure it out and grace when we didn't do things perfectly.

It was a big risk to empower these new believers to teach their peers, but we saw no other way to disciple the hundreds of new believers scattered around the city. We each chose 10 students from the students we had already met with to formulate our own small groups. Each week we taught, trained and discipled those 10 in order for them to, in turn, teach others. We gave focused time to those 60 students we were discipling, and they reached out to the 650 others.

By empowering the students, we saw even more students come to Christ on their campuses and even more in-depth discipleship take place.

To be honest, if I had been in the United States, I would have never entrusted such new believers to disciple others; but in our situation, it was necessary if everyone was to be discipled. We realized that *everyone* is called to "go and make disciples," not just mature believers.

Spiritual Multiplication

This revival happened from 2004 to 2006. As I look back, it's amazing to hear the stories of spiritual multiplication that occurred as we challenged students to continue to share their faith and disciple others around them.

One girl who attended our underground Bible study said that she planned on telling her parents that she had become a Christian. When I asked her if they were Christians, she answered, "No, but I'm sure if I tell them they will believe!" She went back to her village over the winter break and, as a two-month-old believer, led her entire family to the Lord.

A girl we nicknamed Model was invited to the concert by one of the other students. Joey's testimony changed her life and she spent the entire next year being discipled by Ruth in her underground Bible study. She was even baptized in our apartment's bathtub. Unfortunately, after our team came back to America, we lost contact with her.

Several years later, Hannah's dad went to the capital of that country to visit a friend. He was attending his friend's church when a young woman got up in front and shared how believers can systematically share the gospel. Hannah's father knew that someone who served with Cru, formally Campus Crusade for Christ, had trained her because she was training the congregation with the same booklet—*The Four Spiritual Laws*—that the late founder of Cru, Dr. Bill Bright, had written more than 50 years earlier.

After the service, Hannah's dad approached the young woman and asked where she had learned how to share the gospel. She said she had been discipled by an American girl named Hannah, years ago, in another city. Astonished, he pulled out a picture of his daughter, and Model confirmed that his daughter was the one who had discipled her.

Currently, Model is attending seminary in Israel. Her desire is to continue to disciple the people of her home country with the Word of God.

One student we nicknamed Cutie attended Hannah's Bible study and was discipled by her. Cutie was very teachable, so Hannah asked her if she would lead a group of 10 other students and go through the same material that Hannah was teaching her. Cutie was excited to share what she was learning and immediately started teaching a small group and discipling them.

When Cutie learned about the Great Commission (see Matt. 28:18-20) and how the Lord wants us to "go and make disciples," it began to burn in her heart to go to another country after she graduated. She and one of the women she was discipling, Sandy, decided to go serve as missionaries for a year in the Middle East.

Once there, Cutie and Sandy were able to train new believers in that country how to study the Bible, share the gospel and disciple those who came to faith. A year later, they had started a ministry on campus in that predominantly Muslim country.

One day, some Middle Eastern students, who were now going out on campus and openly sharing the gospel with others, met some American college students who attended school at UCLA. These American students were a part of the Navigators, a Christian organization on college campuses throughout America. The American students were overjoyed to see that there were already trained believers on this mostly Muslim campus.

It was clear that these Middle Eastern Christians had been trained via *The Four Spiritual Laws* booklet. The American students from UCLA were curious to hear how they had learned that approach. The Middle Eastern students explained that a year ago two East Asian students, Cutie and Sandy, came to their campus and trained them. Cutie and Sandy had been trained by an American named Hannah, who had discipled them after a band outreach in their city.

Ironically, but no coincidence, Hannah had graduated from UCLA three years before, and some of the Americans knew her. They had heard about the boy band outreach and the revival that occurred in East Asia. When they told the Middle Eastern students that they were friends with Hannah, they were shocked and thrilled.

The Middle Eastern students explained that though they had never met Hannah, they saw her as their spiritual great-grandmother. She had discipled Cutie, who discipled Sandy, who came to the Middle East and discipled them. That was three generations of discipleship all happening within a matter of three years!

We won't know until heaven all that has transpired because the new believers wanted to multiply their lives in others. I am just thankful we took 2 Timothy 2:2 seriously and taught them how to teach others.

MOMENT OF REFLECTION

So we fasted and implored our God for this,
and He listened to our entreaty.
EZRA 8:23

Looking back, our team felt like we were in an impossible situation. We had no clue how we could reach more East Asian students with the gospel under the restrictions of their government. We knew the strategy and wisdom would not come from within ourselves. We needed to seek the wisdom of the Holy Spirit in prayer and fasting for Him to open our eyes to His creative plan.

His plan played out even bigger than we could have imagined. Not only did He want to save the souls of students in our city, but He also wanted them to grow in discipleship and go to other parts of the world to share the gospel with others. We had just wanted to reach students in our city, which seemed impossible in and of itself. But the Lord, in His abundance, used six young adults to train, disciple and send hundreds of students in East Asia back to their families, to their hometowns and to other parts of the world to go and do likewise.

- *The Holy Spirit wants to show us, through prayer and fasting, how He can give us ideas we've never thought of before (see Dan. 9:3-23).*

- *When we trust Him enough to risk trying these inspired ideas, breakthroughs can happen in any stronghold (see 1 Cor. 2:9-13).*

- *We need to follow the guidance of the Holy Spirit even when people may threaten to block our path, like the man did on the last night of the concert (see Acts 19:21–20:1).*

- *We need to realize that prayer and fasting are just as strategic and important as being the person who is physically sharing the gospel with someone.* Not all of us can travel to other parts of the world to be missionaries, but we can pray and fast for God to move in places around the world, and we can still be a part of revival (see Acts 10:30-31).

- *We must be willing to entrust others, even young believers, with the ministry, because they, too, have the wisdom and guidance of the Holy Spirit.* Only then can we see the gospel sent out and more people discipled (see 1 Tim. 4:12).

Questions to Ponder

1. What problem or challenge, which seems impossible to you, can you take to the Lord for wisdom?

2. What might the Spirit be laying upon your heart and mind to pray and fast about? A person? A people group? A country?

3. Who can pray and fast alongside you?

4. What might the Lord be asking you to fast from: Food? Entertainment? TV? For how long?

Holly A. Melton

5. We are all called to "go and make disciples." Is there anyone the Holy Spirit is putting on your heart to disciple? How about someone who might be a little younger in the faith that could benefit from meeting with you, even if it's just once a month?

Conversation with God

1. Share with the Lord things that seem impossible to change or move forward in. Pray in hope and trust that He will guide you in how to make the impossible possible.

2. Ask the Holy Spirit to increase your vision.

3. Daily, carve out a specific time to pray about these things and take time in silence to listen for His voice.

4. During your concentrated time of prayer and fasting, pray through Scripture like Nehemiah 1 and Daniel 9 to guide you on how to pray for others.

5. Ask the Holy Spirit what He wants you, in faith, to do.

6. Pray for revival in the hearts of people, and pray for them to not only receive Jesus but also to share Him with others.

Chapter 7

The Madam's Curse

With the use of cell phones, online chatting and text messaging, we have quicker access to more people than ever before. There are clear advantages and disadvantages to this communication technology. It's wonderful to be able to share something instantly with another person and bring him or her into your world. (Although sometimes on the receiving end it can begin to feel like an intrusion or annoyance if people text or call too often.) Clearly, we need to set some boundaries, but there are times when we need to be willing to have our agendas interrupted because God has a different plan for that moment.

Motel Madness

My agenda got interrupted one night in Santa Monica, California, while I was hanging out with a group of college students. These students had just finished spending 10 weeks learning how to share their faith with others, and this was their last night together.

They were all living together in a rundown motel that also had a handful of permanent residents living among them. We had brought in bunk beds and managed to stuff four people into closet-sized rooms. Though the motel needed a facelift, the energy was explosive as the students made the motel their own.

Carports were turned into hangout areas they decorated with free sofas found around town. They strung white Christmas lights around the poles. Artwork they had painted hung on the dingy walls. They had made the best of it, and the dumpy motel became their home away from home.

The students didn't just stick to themselves, though. When they came home from work or ministry outreaches, they would hang out with the residents who lived there. Most of the residents were just one step away from living on the streets. Not having friends or much of a social life, they welcomed the students into their lives.

Endearingly, the students nicknamed the permanent residents "permies." The permies enjoyed the students' youthful energy and would often come out to join them in games, singing or conversations.

This last night was different. It had a more serious feel to it. Tomorrow they would go their separate ways to their various campuses to start a new year. They had gone from strangers, 10 weeks before, to lifelong friends, and they didn't want their night of fellowship to end.

In the middle of one of the students' sharing what she had learned over the summer, one of the permies, Debbie, came out of her room clothed in her shabby bathrobe, frantically screaming.

Debbie was a unique individual. She housed a little zoo in her crowded motel room. She had an iguana that was more than three feet long; eight stray cats; three hamsters that rolled around in clear balls; a tank full of colorful fish; and a raccoon she rescued after he was hit by a car. We had no clue how she had room for all of those little critters. We definitely preferred hanging out with her outside, because her room just smelled too much like animal urine, and fur was caked on the carpet and bedding.

We also learned that Debbie's pattern was to sleep during the day, as every evening she'd come out to hang with the students in her threadbare robe, having just awakened. Tonight, something was different. She ran out of her room in such a frenzy that all of us immediately redirected our attention to her flailing body heading in our direction.

As she ran up to us, she cried out in gasps, "You're Christians, right? I'm so scared! A woman who worked for me, that I just fired, said that she was a witch and she put a curse on me! Can she do that? I'm so scared! How do I stop it? What can I do?"

The students looked at her, bug-eyed and in silence. That's when I knew tonight was no longer going to be about my agenda. I needed to pull Debbie aside and listen to her situation.

As I stood up—albeit a little reluctantly—from my cozy seat on the couch in the carport, I turned to the student beside me and asked her to pray. I gently grabbed Debbie's shaking arm and encouraged her to walk with me to another part of the driveway where we could talk more personally.

He Is Greater

As we sat in two rusty folding chairs underneath the motel's neon lights, I touched her arm and said, "Okay, Debbie. Let's calm down so that you can talk to me and tell me what happened. Breathe . . . just breathe . . . good . . ."

Debbie finally said, "I had to fire her. She wasn't working. She was so mad at me on the phone. That's when she told me she had special powers, because she's a witch. She said she put a curse on me and my animals, and to watch out. I hung up the phone as fast as I could, and that's when I ran outside. I just wanted to get out of there. When I'm around you all I feel safe."

Still rubbing her arm lightly, I bent forward and calmly said, "There is a way you can know you will be safe."

"There is?! What is it?"

"Well, first of all, you said that you feel safe around us, the Christians. Why do you think that is?"

"I don't know. Everyone just seems so happy and loving. It's like they know they are safe because of God or something. And I don't have that."

At that moment, the Holy Spirit gave me a verse to share with her that totally related to what she was experiencing. "Have you heard of this before?" I asked. "The book of 1 John 4:4 tells us, 'He who is in you is greater than he who is in the world.'"

She shook her head no.

"Would you like me to explain it to you and how it relates to your situation?" She nodded yes, and I continued. "When it says, 'He who is in you,' it is talking about God's Spirit being placed inside of us when we believe in Jesus. When His Spirit comes inside us, He is a seal of protection from an eternity separated from God, and protection from the evil one, Satan, who is roaming this earth. The verse is declaring that God's Spirit who is inside of Christians is greater and more powerful than the forces of Satan and his followers on the earth. But for those who only know *about* Jesus and have not yet invited him into their lives, the Spirit is not protecting them, and curses *can* be placed on them.

"In light of this, the first question you must ask yourself is, 'Have I ever placed my faith in Jesus as my Lord and Savior?' This is the only way to be protected from the evil forces around us."

Debbie said she had invited Jesus into her life years before. It seemed hard to believe, but it wasn't my role to judge if she had or hadn't. I asked the Holy Spirit to show me what passage of Scripture to go through with her to clarify the gospel, even though she might be a believer.

Preparing for Battle

The passage the Spirit put on my mind was about spiritual warfare, found in chapter 6 of the book of Ephesians. I wanted her to grasp how God protects us with the armor of God, which is essentially putting on the truth of the gospel every day.

I had never read this passage as an evangelistic approach, but it just seemed to fit the situation perfectly. I love how the Holy Spirit is so creative when we are willing to use the Word of God in people's lives.

I asked Debbie if I could read to her a few verses and see if it seemed to fit her situation. She nodded, so I opened my Bible and began to read:

Finally, be strong in the Lord and in the strength of His might. Put on the whole armor of God, that you may be able to stand against the schemes of the devil. For we do not wrestle against flesh and blood, but against the rulers, against the authorities, against the cosmic powers over this present darkness, against the spiritual forces of evil in the heavenly places. Therefore take up the whole armor of God, that you may be able to withstand in the evil day, and having done all, to stand firm (Eph. 6:10-13).

"According to this passage, Debbie, who are we fighting against?"

"Spiritual forces of evil?"

"Correct. You're not fighting the woman you fired, but the forces in which she is getting her power. So how do we battle against these spiritual forces and schemes of the devil, according to this passage?"

"By putting on God's armor?"

"Exactly. Would you like to know what that is so you can stand firm against these evil forces?"

"Of course!"

"All right! Then let's keep reading! 'Stand therefore, having fastened on the belt of truth, and having put on the breastplate of righteousness, and, as shoes for your feet, having put on the readiness given by the gospel of peace' (v. 14). What do you think the belt of truth is that you fasten on?"

"God?"

"Yes. More specifically, it is what God says in His Word, in the Bible. You see, Satan is called 'the father of lies,' and he can easily deceive us to believe things that are not true about God or about ourselves and other people. For example, Satan wants you to believe that he is more powerful than God, but he's not. He wants you to believe that you are powerless against his curse, but you are not if you have Jesus in your life. The only way we can know this truth and fasten it tightly to our beings is if we read the Bible, study it and allow it to change the way we think about God, ourselves and others. Does that make sense?"

"Yes. To be honest, I have a Bible, but I've never read it."

"That's okay. You can start now! I will show you later where you can start in the book of John to learn more about Jesus and who He is. Now back to this verse. It goes on to say that we are to put on a 'breastplate of righteousness.' A breastplate helps protect our most vital organs, like our heart and lungs. So understanding the term 'righteousness' is vital for us to survive these spiritual battles. What do you think righteousness means?"

"I don't know. I've never really heard this word other than saying someone is acting righteous, or better than others. Is that what it means? We must think we are better than Satan?"

"Well, not exactly, but I see how you can think that. Righteousness is not something we are; it is the way God sees us. Let me explain. Jesus is the only person who was righteous. He was the only one who lived on this earth and never sinned. Because of that, He could be in the presence of God the Father. This allowed them to have an intimate relationship.

"We, on the other hand, are not naturally righteous. We've been sinning since the day we were born! And because of that, we cannot be in God's presence and protection, and we are not naturally in a relationship with Him. The reason Jesus had to die on the cross was so that His righteousness, His perfect standing with God, could be offered to us.

"When we believe in Jesus as our Lord and Savior, His right standing before God, or His righteousness, becomes ours. This is called God's grace, because we are given an opportunity to be in a right relationship with God even though we don't deserve it. And when we have a relationship with God, He can fully protect us from the enemy. Having this righteousness of Jesus placed on us is vital to protecting us. Does this make sense?"

"Yes. So what else do we need to put on?"

"Well, it also says that for our feet we need to put on the 'gospel of peace.' The gospel is just what I shared, that Jesus died on the cross for our sins so that we can believe in Him and have a right relationship with God. When we know that we are right with God, and we don't have to live in fear of His condemnation, then we can live in peace, even if Satan and his evil forces are against us. We know that we are with the Most Powerful One."

Her Secret Past

After sharing this, Debbie looked down and offered, "I do live in fear of God's condemnation. I have not lived a good life. No one here knows what I do for a living. If they knew, they probably wouldn't even be my friends."

"That's not true, Debbie. We love you."

"What if I were to tell you that in my younger years I was a porn star? I filmed porn movies for 12 years. Obviously, I'm too old for that now, but I've been so intertwined in the industry. I feel like people judge those of us who have been in the porn industry, even though it's not hurting anyone. It's just a form of entertainment."

As I looked into Debbie's beautiful blue eyes, I tried to imagine what she might have looked like 30 years ago. In front of me I only saw a woman with graying hair that severely needed to be brushed; a body that hadn't exercised in years; a face of deep crevices, probably enhanced from her chain smoking.

In compassion, I reached out for her hands and said, "Debbie, no matter what you've done or are doing now, I care about you. I may not agree that pornography doesn't negatively affect people, but I still care about you very much."

"Why do you say it negatively affects people?" she asked. "How can watching videos be harmful?"

I pointed to the group of students hanging out near us and said, "You see those boys over there? They want to follow Jesus so badly. But when they get on the Internet, they are quickly confronted with scandalous pictures of women. Most of them, if not all of them, have struggled with pornography. And now, here on this summer project, they are trying so hard to not look at the women here in a lustful way."

Debbie looked at me, shocked. "To think that these sweet Christian boys I met all summer could struggle because of the industry I am a part of seems unimaginable."

"You see, Debbie, the porn industry is enticing for those who are creating the porn, as well as for those who are watching it. And unfortunately, in the end, both the people who work in the industry and those who observe porn become enslaved. It affects all of their lives in serious ways."

Holly A. Melton

Her head bowed low in shame. A sniffle came from under her hooded robe, and she asked, "How can I be forgiven for *that*?"

"Debbie, God can forgive you even for that. Jesus died for *all* of our sins. No sin is too big for Him to cover. Let's keep reading and see what the rest of the armor is. I think it will encourage you.

"It says in verse 16, 'In all circumstances take up the shield of faith, with which you can extinguish all the flaming darts of the evil one; and take the helmet of salvation, and the sword of the Spirit, which is the word of God, praying at all times in the Spirit, with all prayer and supplication.' The shield of faith seems pretty important if you feel like Satan is attacking you. What do you think faith means here?"

"Faith that God will protect me?"

"Yes. Faith means believing in something you can't see or feel. Sometimes it might not feel like God is more powerful, but He is. We need to have faith that He can conquer the enemy and protect us from evil. What about the helmet? Why is that called 'salvation'?"

"Does the helmet save us?" she asked.

"Sort of. The helmet protects our brain—our mind, right? So the helmet of salvation can remind us that Satan cannot hear our thoughts. He cannot control our minds, because being saved by Jesus protects us. Nothing can take away our salvation. Even after we accept Jesus into our life, we still sin. When we do, Satan might want us to doubt that God loves us, or doubt that we can be forgiven; and ultimately he wants us to doubt that we are saved. When you put on this helmet, it reminds you that you are saved because of what Jesus has done for you, not what you have done for Him. Does this make sense?"

Debbie said yes.

"Okay, well let's look at our weapon. Any soldier that has a weapon must learn how to use it and believe that it can protect him or her and destroy the enemy. This weapon is to help us on the offense, not the defense, as in the case of a shield, helmet or breastplate. So what is the one weapon we are given?"

"The sword of the Spirit," Debbie replied, "which is the Word of God."

"Yes! The sword is not just a book; it is the actual words of God that are still alive today. When we accept Jesus as our Savior, we are given His Spirit inside of us. We talked about this earlier with the verse found in the book of John. The Spirit teaches us truth when we read the Word of God. We can then speak out this truth to fight against the enemy.

"Satan loses all power and authority when we speak out the truth found in the Word of God. If we say Satan has no power because the Bible says he has no power, then his power is taken away from him. If we say, 'He who is in me is greater than he who is in the world,' then Satan must back down because that word is truth. Does using the Word of God as a weapon make sense?"

Debbie responded, "So, when I think about the woman who tried to put a curse on me, I do not need to be afraid if I believe Jesus' righteousness has covered me and I am in a right relationship with God. If I am in a right relationship with God, then I can use the Spirit that is within me to help me speak truth from the Word of God to fight the enemy and make him powerless. Is that how it works?"

"Wow! Exactly!" I was so excited, because it seemed like Debbie was really grasping the gospel as well as how to fight against the spiritual forces battling around her. I looked at her and said, "How does all of this make you feel?"

She was silent for a moment and then said, "Well, I haven't been totally honest with you. You don't know what I do now for a living . . ."

Her Secret Present

To be honest, I just wanted to roll my eyes at her and say, "*Now* what?!" We'd been talking for almost two hours, it was getting late and I wanted to hang out with the students. Instead of rolling my eyes, I asked the Spirit to give me patience and to continue to ask questions and listen. I knew this night was not about me, and I needed to stay engaged with her for as long as the Spirit guided me.

"Debbie, I can't enter in and understand your situation unless you are honest with me. What do you do for a living?"

"Well, it's illegal. That's why I live here at this motel and don't tell people what I do. I work as a madam. I organize a whole network of prostitutes in major cities around the country through the Internet." Then her voice became frantic and she said, "Do you think I'm being punished because of what I do? Does God hate me? I just don't know how to make money doing anything else!"

Was I really having this conversation? Was she for real? In my naiveté, I didn't even know people could get prostitutes online. *How does one even discover a job like hers?*

As if she read my mind, she answered, "Porn stars and prostitution often go hand in hand. Sometimes the women do both. As I got older, I began to be like a mother to many of the younger women in the porn industry. Many of them had children they had to provide for. Others had addictions they had to feed. The porn industry didn't pay enough, especially as the Internet got more global and people could view porn for free. So prostitution, though more degrading, was a way to use the commodity they knew they had, their bodies, to make a lot more money than they ever dreamed.

"I started to have women beg me to help them become prostitutes. I quickly established a network of women by sending them to various cities around the country. In fact, the reason I keep checking my phone during our conversation is to see if there are any more appointments that need to be arranged."

I took a deep breath and slowly released it as I asked the Spirit to give me His words to say. "Debbie, God loves anyone who turns from their ways to follow Him. It is sad that so many of these women feel hopeless and do not see another option for work. Have you heard the story of the prostitute who approached Jesus with her most expensive perfume?"

"No. I didn't even know there was a story of Jesus and a prostitute."

"There is. It's found in Luke, chapter 7. This woman, known as 'a woman of the city'" (Luke 7:37) went to Jesus while He was dining with His disciples. She took an expensive flask of ointment and poured it on His feet. The disciples thought it was a disgrace for Jesus to allow this 'sinner' to be touching Him.

"Jesus rebuked them and said that because she grasped His forgiveness toward her, she loved Him greatly and was displaying her love to Him by washing His feet with her tears and pouring the oil onto Him. She knew He would love and care for her if she trusted Him, so she wanted to give Him everything she had. Though the men around her saw her as a sinner, Jesus saw her as forgiven. And Jesus can do the same for you.

"You don't need to stay in the career you are working in, Debbie, and neither do the women who are working for you. But first, you must trust Jesus enough to surrender your life to Him, wanting to leave behind anything that dishonors Him. God doesn't hate you, but He won't bless your sin. Could you surrender your job to Jesus and trust Him to provide you with a better work situation?"

"I want His love and forgiveness so badly!" she replied. "I'd even be willing to leave this career if I knew the women I let go could get other jobs as well."

The Holy Spirit then brought to my mind the story of the Israelites who were slaves in Egypt, and how I could parallel their situation to Debbie's. I said, "God wanted to free the Israelites from slavery in Egypt and take them to the Promised Land, but first they had to trust that He would provide for them if they left Egypt.

"Then, on the journey through the desert, they'd have to trust that their future situation would be better than their past situation, which felt comfortable to them even though they were in slavery. God couldn't change their circumstances unless they were first willing to leave a place that was known, familiar and comfortable.

"That is the same with you and the women who work for you. God wants to free you from this career and the bondage it creates, but you'll have to leave without knowing the future, trusting that in your obedience, God will provide you with a better future that is more honoring to Him."

Debbie looked at me with a glimmer of mischief in her eyes and said, "Are you my Moses? Did God bring you into my life to help free me from this lifestyle I have been in for more than 35 years? Did He bring you to guide me from a life of shame and bondage to a life of hope and joy? I am ready. The time has been long overdue for me to surrender my life to Jesus."

With a huge smile on both of our faces, Debbie surrendered her life and her lifestyle to the Lord. She said she would trust Him with her future and how to be a better influence to the women she had hired to be prostitutes for her.

God Froze the Internet

The next afternoon, after the students had tearfully said their good-byes and headed home, I knocked on Debbie's door to see how she was doing. As she opened the door with her raccoon on her shoulder, she said, "God froze the Internet last night! God froze the Internet!"

"What do you mean, 'God froze the Internet'?"

"Well, after you left, I prayed for about 20 minutes, just surrendering all that I could think of to the Lord. I felt this peace flood over me and my situation. The phone rang at 2:00 AM, interrupting me. It was one of my girls who works for me in Texas. She said the Internet was down and she wasn't able to see if she had any more clients that night. So I went to the Internet, thinking it was just her connection, but I discovered that *my* Internet was down. So I called another girl who lives in Washington, and *her* Internet was frozen as well. I'm telling you, God froze the Internet last night at 2:00 AM! There was no Internet again until around 5:30 this morning!

"The only way I can make sense of it is that I surrendered my work to the Lord and the girls I've hired; and in response, He stopped their work for the night. No one got to their appointments after 2:00 AM. It just confirmed to me that I was making the right decision and that God wants this for me and the girls! I know it seems crazy, but I can't wait to call each of them and share with them about the love and power of God! They may not accept it, but I'm praying they'll at least listen to me."

I shook my head in amazement. "Debbie," I said with a smile, "I would have never thought of God stopping the Internet from working so that His plan could be accomplished. But why not? He's God! That's incredible! Can you believe it was just last night that you came out frantic that a curse had been placed on you, and now you have hope, peace, joy and a new confidence in God that you haven't had before? God has an amazing plan for you!"

Debbie's eyes sparkled, and she thanked me for listening to her and challenging her to take the step of faith to leave her "Egypt." She was ready for the new adventure ahead, and she couldn't wait to bring the women she'd led along with her.

MOMENT OF REFLECTION

He who is in you is greater than he who is in the world.
1 JOHN 4:4

Though this conversation took longer in real life than it takes to read on paper, I am still amazed how quickly Debbie grasped some of the deep truths of the gospel. Before I met Debbie, if you were to ask me how to share the gospel with someone in the porn industry, or someone involved with prostitution, or someone who's walking through spiritual warfare, I would have said, "I have no clue." As I reflect on my conversation with Debbie, I am reminded that Christians don't have to know what they are going to say to be open to talking with someone who is very different from them.

We learn what to say by listening to and walking with the Holy Spirit and letting Him lead us in the conversation. We cannot compartmentalize people in such a way that we decide we aren't skilled enough to share Jesus with that "type" of person. That mindset is truly insulting to the story of the gospel and the power of the Holy Spirit in our lives. The truth is:

• *The Spirit might want to use us at moments when we wish we were doing something else.* We must continually ask the Holy Spirit to give us patience and focus to stay engaged with a person for as long as He wants us to. We must surrender our own agenda and submit to His (see Acts 16:6-7).

• *When we ask the Holy Spirit to guide us, He gives us wisdom about the spiritual world and how to talk to others about it.* Remember, He *is* greater than any spiritual forces around us (see Eph. 6:10-20).

• *The Holy Spirit shows us what Scriptures relate to the person with whom we are engaging so that we can bring him or her to Jesus.* If you aren't as familiar with the stories of Jesus, I'd encourage you to read through the gospels. Think about how Jesus' interactions with others in the Bible can relate to people around you today. Bringing stories of Jesus to others is a way for them to see that He has already engaged with a person similar to them.

• *The Holy Spirit wants us to lovingly challenge others to live a life of surrender, because Jesus should be our Lord, not just our Savior.* Debbie thought she believed in Jesus. I never told her she didn't, but I led her to understand the need for surrender. Often, we are afraid to ask people to surrender things in their lives. It is true that God loves the sinner but hates the sin. It is true that when we come to Jesus, we will not be perfect, nor will we grasp the depth of our sin. But if a person doesn't grasp that he or she should live a life of surrender from the start, it is unlikely that we will see that person's life change (see Acts 21:11-14).

Questions to Ponder

1. Have you been willing to allow the Holy Spirit to interrupt your agenda if He wants you to engage with someone in the moment? Why or why not? Are you able to put everything else to the side and focus on the moment? What can help you to do this better?

2. Have you ever experienced spiritual warfare? If so, how did you feel? How did you walk through it? What principles can you apply to your own life when you think through the armor of God in Ephesians 6?

3. How well do you know the stories found in the gospels about Jesus? Would you be able to see how various people to whom Jesus related back then could represent types of people you engage with now?

4. Have *you* been living a life of surrender? It's a daily decision made with humility and determination.

Conversation with God

1. Praise God that He is greater than any evil forces that try to defeat us.

2. Pray through Ephesians 6 and put on the full armor of God so that you can stand firm against the schemes of the evil one.

3. Pray to be available when the Holy Spirit wants to use you, and that you'd be flexible with your agenda.

4. Ask the Holy Spirit to give you insight on how the accounts in the gospels could relate to others you come into contact with.

5. Ask the Holy Spirit if there are things you need to surrender to Him, and then take the time to humbly surrender these things at the foot of the cross.

Chapter 8

Buried Treasure, an Auction and My Neighbors

Maybe we weren't all raised in the same generation, but I remember watching *Mr. Rogers' Neighborhood* on TV in the mornings, wondering what it would be like to be Mr. Rogers's neighbor. He had such a warm, welcoming voice. He would walk slowly around the living room, smile into the camera and even put on his cozy red sweater as he sang to his television audience this song about wanting to be "my" neighbor:

> *It's a beautiful day in this neighborhood,*
> *A beautiful day for a neighbor,*
> *Would you be mine?*
> *Could you be mine?*

When we think about our neighbors, we may not be saying, "I've always wanted to have a neighbor *just like you*," but I like how Mr. Rogers challenges us with the line, "So, let's make the most of this beautiful day, since we're together, we might as well say . . .

won't you be my neighbor?" Not to dig too deeply on a theme song from a kid's show, but there's something to that song that makes us long for community. We were made to live in community. I don't think that means just our immediate families, or our church communities, but the community in which we live.

The second greatest commandment, after loving the Lord, is to "love your neighbor as yourself" (Matt. 22:39). I know I spend a lot of time loving and caring for myself. What if I took just a little time to start loving my neighbors? What could happen?

The challenge is that the American culture has changed. Our society is more fast-paced than in the past. We no longer sit on our porch to watch the sunset while talking to our neighbors across the street. We don't offer a home-cooked meal when the U-haul truck shows up down the road with a young family moving in. We don't remember our neighbors' first names, so when our paths cross on the sidewalk, we might wave, smile, mumble "Hi," then keep walking by. Maybe we stop and chat for a moment, but the conversation never gets very deep.

How do you build a relationship with your neighbors if they're still strangers? Maybe it's time to step up to their door and sing Mr. Rogers's song (not literally!). Or maybe it's time to ask the Holy Spirit how you should enter into your neighbors' lives, one opportunity at a time.

Our Jerusalem

After Jesus rose from the dead, He had one final declaration to share with His disciples: "When the Holy Spirit has come upon you . . . you will be my witnesses in Jerusalem and in all Judea and Samaria, and to the end of the earth" (Acts 1:8). This message is for us as well. He wants us to make an impact on the whole world, but we are to start out in our "Jerusalem," which is our own city, community or town. Let's even narrow that down to our neighborhood, street or next-door neighbors. If we are going to start somewhere, and we should, the place to start is with the people who live around us.

After I came back from living in East Asia, I wanted to live out this verse by focusing on my Jerusalem. I felt like I had gone "to the ends of the earth," but what was I doing to meet my neighbors?

Buried Treasure

I was in the process of looking for a place to live by driving around and writing down phone numbers of apartment complexes in Southern California. One day, I had mistaken a condo complex for an apartment complex, so I called a realtor rather than an apartment manager. While on the phone with her, she suggested I do some research and see if I could get a loan from my bank to buy a home. The idea seemed unrealistic since I was a single woman serving in a nonprofit, vocational ministry, which brought in around the same salary as a teacher. How could I afford anything in California? The answer was, I couldn't.

When I got a call back from the loan officer, he said *all* I would need is a down payment of $30,000. As if $30,000 was only a drop in the bucket! I didn't have that sort of savings account, so with a sigh, I replied, "Thanks, anyway," and hung up the phone. I slowly walked to the bathroom, hoping that a hot shower would wash away my disappointment.

When I got out of the shower, I saw that I had a voicemail on my cell phone. It was from a couple that had supported me and my ministry for the past eight years. I couldn't believe my ears when the man said that God put me on his heart that morning during his prayer time. He felt the Holy Spirit prodding him to give me 2,000 antique Canadian coins he had buried in his back yard. I felt both confused and excited as my mind tried to process this strange message. I called him back immediately.

Once again, he shared with me how he felt prodded by the Spirit to give me these coins. I asked how much they were worth. He replied, "We'd have to get them appraised and sell them at a coin collector's shop, but I'd say they are worth around $28,000."

"What? Really? Twenty-eight thousand dollars?! May I share with you the phone call I had just before you left me a voicemail?"

I explained the opportunity to possibly buy a condo if I had $30,000 for a down payment. I asked if he felt like that was a good use of his gift to me, and he said that it most certainly was. If I was able to get into the housing market, he thought I should go for it.

After talking to him briefly about next steps, I got off the phone and just started to cry. I had never thought I could afford my own place, especially as a single female missionary serving in California. I was now on the journey to find my Jerusalem.

The Auction

The worship leader at my church was my realtor. Our search for the perfect condo was disappointing because each place seemed to need a lot of renovations, which I didn't have the budget for. Then, one day online, I saw this little ad for a condo community that was recently renovated and would be selling at an auction in a few weeks. I had no clue how to buy a home at an auction, so I attended a one-hour training on the process.

It all seemed so overwhelming. I just didn't have time to research everything about buying a house. The prayer I kept praying over and over again was, "Lord, if it is Your will for me to own my own place, please provide a condo in the community You want me to live in. If it is not Your will for me to own at this time, or this is not the community You want me to live in, then please protect me by not giving me a condo in this auction." The two key words were "provide" and "protect." I wanted to know that either way the decision would be the Lord's.

One tip I learned from the one-hour auction training was to get to the auction early and sit in the front row, directly across from the auctioneer. The auction was held in a conference room at a Doubletree in Anaheim. Every person had to present a $5,000 check just to enter the room. My realtor, Nick, and I walked in early and sat in the front row. Nick tried to help me be realistic by explaining, "Just remember, it's very unlikely you'll get a condo today. Look at how many people are in the room—at least 500! I just don't want you to be too disappointed if it doesn't work out."

I appreciated his care and concern, but without hesitation, I replied, "Let's have faith. Maybe God wants to provide today. Maybe He wants to protect me. Either way, I trust Him. I will not leave disappointed if I don't get a condo. I will trust it wasn't the right place or timing. But let's still have faith going into this auction." I then excused myself to go use the restroom and have a few minutes alone before the auction began.

Grant Me Favor

The whole auction process seemed way over my head. As I headed to the restroom, I began to pray. I felt the Holy Spirit's prompting to pray like Nehemiah did before he went before the king. He said in his prayer in Nehemiah 1:11, "Grant me success today by making the king favorable to me" (*NLT*). I'd never prayed a pray for favor or success before, but I stopped and prayed, "Okay, Lord. I ask for You to please grant me favor before the auctioneer today, whatever that may look like, just like You granted Nehemiah favor before the king. I trust You. Amen." As I walked back to my seat, I felt a flood of peace rush over me as the auctioneer took his place on the stand.

Each condo I bid on was trumped by bids up to $60,000 over my budget. I looked around the room as poster numbers kept flying up from buyers' hands, and a profound thought came to me. If I get a condo here today, my neighbors will be people sitting in this room. A new prayer came to my mind as I sat in the front row: "Lord, if You want me to live in this community, with people in this room, please prepare their hearts to want to hear about You. Have people buy these condos that You want me to befriend and share You with." I had an immediate purpose that if I were to move in to this community, with these very people, I had confidence that God would be pursuing their hearts. It would be a community handpicked by God.

Chosen

The first 15 condos that were sold were well over my budget. As I held my poster number up high for the next condo up for bid, I was shocked when the auctioneer pointed right at me and said to the crowd of people, "Give this woman a house already!"

What?! I couldn't believe it! If Nick hadn't been with me, I would have thought I was dreaming it. The auctioneer had given me direct favor! I am sure he could have lost his job for this one random act of kindness. Miraculously, no one bid over me, and I won the sixteenth condo at the auction.

Nick and I stood up in a daze as we were escorted to another room where I would begin signing papers. Tears welled up in my eyes. As I sat down at a small table, I looked around the room at the other 15 people who were signing papers. They were going to be my neighbors. My smile felt like it had the power to crack my face as I realized that God had given me an incredible gift. No doubt, He wanted me to get to know these individuals seated around me and love on them.

No matter where you live, whether it's at home with your parents, in a dorm room on campus, in an apartment complex in the city, or on a farm in the middle of a small rural town, you are called to be a witness in your Jerusalem, the community around you. It will look different for each of us, but we must begin to get to know our neighbors. And that's exactly what I did.

Getting to Know You

Looking back, I remember meeting my neighbors the day I moved in. I was carrying boxes from my friend's pick-up truck when a car pulled into the cobblestone driveway and a man rolled down his window. With a thick accent and a wonderful smile, he said hello and asked about the condos. I told him it was a pleasant place to live; that it was a gated community, a quiet environment and had a pool. I felt safe here, and it felt like home. After our brief dialogue, I remember his blonde wife thanking me from the passenger's side before they drove off. This was my first interaction with Alex and Naomi.

About a month later, I saw them outside my window as they were moving in. They had bought the condo below me. I felt nervous to meet them, so I prayed and asked the Spirit to fill me and give me the words to say to start building a relationship with them.

When I went downstairs to introduce myself, I learned that Alex was from Afghanistan and Naomi was from Romania. I have always enjoyed learning about other cultures, so over the next few months, I spent hours with them looking at their family pictures on Facebook and learning about what it was like to be raised in Romania and Afghanistan. Sometimes I didn't know what questions to ask, but every time I asked the Spirit to guide the conversation, I felt like we got to know each other on a deeper, more intimate level.

Entering into Their Joy

Just like many couples that live in California, they both needed to work in order to pay the mortgage. Naomi told me she was looking for a job, but work seemed to be scarce. I touched her shoulder and said I would pray that God would provide her with a job. A few weeks later, she found work only a few blocks from where we lived. I felt like the Holy Spirit wanted me to find a way to enter into her joy, so I bought her a bouquet of flowers.

She shared with me later that she was so surprised that a neighbor would do such a kind act as to get her flowers. She admitted that, at first, she thought there was a catch, an expectation that she'd need to do something in return; but she was pleasantly surprised when she learned I just wanted to enter into her joy.

Being a Blessing

One day when I came to visit, Naomi was all giddy; she shared with me that she was pregnant! Since I didn't know any of her friends, and her friends didn't really know her neighbors, I didn't think at the time about hosting a baby shower for her. Around her eighth month of pregnancy, I asked if anyone at either of her two jobs was throwing a baby shower for her. She shook her head, a little sadly it seemed to me, and said no. As I look back, I wish I had thought more about that and how I could have blessed her by host-ing one.

I figured the least I could do this late in her pregnancy was shower her with baby gifts. When my friends at church heard that my neighbor was pregnant but didn't get a shower, they bought her some cute outfits and even offered bags of adorable used clothing. Naomi couldn't believe that people would bless her like that when they didn't even know her. It blessed me, as well, to see people choose to give and love someone they had never met.

Naomi's mom decided to come from Romania when the baby, Joel, was born. Living with them, she was able to help care for Joel when Naomi headed back to work. Naomi's mother, Mary, spoke no English, so we often talked to each other via Naomi interpreting. Since Mary was home most of the time, I'd often wave at her through the kitchen window. I knew I could at least wave, smile and say, "Hi, Mary!" and be friendly.

Experiencing Jesus Together

It was the beginning of December, and I didn't want the season to go by without inviting some of my neighbors to hear the story of Je-sus. I asked the Holy Spirit to show me what I could invite them to go see that would help engage them with the real meaning of Christmas.

My roommate informed me that a church nearby was hosting a free musical. I invited Mary and Naomi, along with another neighbor of mine, Angela, who was from a Buddhist background. All three of them joined me and seemed to have a wonderful time. Since English wasn't the native language for any of them, we revis-ited the storyline on the ride home and had a great discussion on what they each knew about Jesus and His life.

I invited them to my church for a Christmas service. Angela would be with her family that evening, but Naomi said her whole family wanted to come, including Alex and Joel. Though Alex was from a Muslim background, he seemed to enjoy holding his young son on his knee and bouncing him to the beat of the Christmas music.

After the service, we gathered in the lobby for a picture by the Christmas tree, and then headed to the car. As we walked, Alex explained to me that he believed Jesus was a prophet. I told him I agreed, the Bible says He was a prophet. Alex then said he believed we worship the same god, even if our religions were different.

We didn't get the opportunity to go deeper with the conversation because we had reached the car, but I prayed that the Spirit would work in each of their lives as they continued to learn more of who Jesus was and is.

A Humbling Proposal

Before I drove to Arizona to spend Christmas with my family, I stopped by the next day to give Alex's family some little gifts. While there, Naomi said they had wanted to ask me something but didn't know how to ask me, so they had been putting it off. I told her she never had to be nervous to ask me anything. She then said, "Would you be willing to be Joel's godmother?"

Naomi was raised partially Catholic and partially Orthodox Christian. She didn't really have clarity on what she believed, but she felt like it was important for her child to have a godparent. I wondered how Alex felt about me being the godparent of their firstborn son. I knew that without his blessing, I couldn't even consider it. I looked over at Alex and said, "Are you sure you want me to be the godmother of your son? I am Christian; you are Muslim. Naomi is sort of Catholic/Christian. A godparent is usually a person who influences the child's life spiritually. Is that what you are looking for?"

Alex looked at me and without hesitation replied, "There is no one else we'd rather have teach our son about God." *Wow.* A Muslim man from the Middle East wanted me to teach his son about God. It was incredible, humbling and dumbfounding, all at the same time. I looked at each of them in the eye before I said, "Well, then, yes, I'd be honored to be Joel's godmother. Thank you for considering me for this significant role in his life."

That night, as I lay in bed, I prayed that the Holy Spirit would fall on them; that God would reveal Himself to them in an intimate way; that He'd show me how to be a spiritual influence to Joel and a spiritual strength for the whole family. I prayed that they would come to know Jesus personally and be able to raise their son with godly wisdom and direction. As tears rolled down my cheeks onto my pillow, I thanked the Lord for choosing me for such a humbling role. Then, I drifted off to sleep.

Homeowners Association

I attended our quarterly HOA (homeowners association) meetings so that I could get to know my neighbors and be involved in what was happening within our condo community. This is where I began to grow my friendship with my neighbor Angela. After getting a divorce, she moved here from Taiwan to live closer to her grown-up children. Though traditionally a Buddhist, she said that her son and daughter-in-law went to church and she sometimes went with them. I was encouraged to hear that she had believers in her family. I prayed that the Holy Spirit would show me how I, too, could be a part of her spiritual journey in learning more about Jesus.

That opportunity arose after months of me sitting and listening to her fears and concerns about the HOA. Angela was our treasurer because she was gifted at analyzing the budget and finances of our association. She wanted to make sure that every financial decision was wise and legal. It seemed that she didn't trust the management company's records of how money was being spent. Over time, this brought her great stress and began to affect her health.

I invited her over for dinner one evening to talk through her role on the board and how it was affecting her. Before the meal, I asked if I could say a prayer, and she said sure. "Lord, thank You for giving us a home to live in. Thank You for wonderful neighbors. Thank You that You will provide for us in these challenging economic times and that You will protect us from fraud and evil as we seek You. Thank You that You know us, our fears, anxieties and stresses, and that You can help us find peace despite our circumstances. Thank You that we can trust You. Thank You for this food and good fellowship. Please guide our conversation over dinner, and give us wisdom. Amen."

As we began to eat, Angela admitted that she had never thought about God being in control of these sorts of things, and she never thought of praying about it. "In Buddhism," she explained, "you just pray to Buddha for good health or prosperity. We don't pray in specifics about a situation."

"Oh," I replied. "I hadn't known how one prays to Buddha. What did you think about how I prayed to God?"

"It seemed more natural, more comfortable . . . more relational."

"Yes. I believe it's because God wants to be relational with us. In fact, that is why He sent His only Son, Jesus, to die. Without Jesus' death, we could not have a personal, intimate relationship with God. I don't know about you, but I know I am far from perfect, and so for God to associate with me, I needed to find a way to be right before Him. No matter how loving or good I try to be, I am still selfish at my core, and so I realized I needed Jesus as my personal Savior to save me from my selfish self.

"Once I made that decision, my perspective on life changed. People may hurt me and cheat me, and maybe the HOA management company is even doing that. I don't know. But I do know that God will guide and protect me as I seek Him."

Angela listened, but I wasn't sure she was fully grasping what I was trying to explain. Instead of replying, she changed the topic to share that she was considering stepping down from the HOA board. I knew that the Spirit wanted me to follow the flow of the conversation and not try to lead her to a point of decision. So I asked her if I could pray for her and her health, and she said she'd like that.

After we prayed, she asked if I would join the board if she stepped down. I laughed and told her I'd pray about it. A few months later, it was time to vote in new board members, and I was voted in to take her place. I knew this would help encourage me to continue to care about the community I lived in and help me to get to know my neighbors.

A Frightening Pregnancy

About a year and a half after Joel was born, Naomi was pregnant with their second child. Partway through the pregnancy she had some bleeding and was rushed to the hospital. This was a time for me to enter in and be there for her and her family, but I wasn't sure how. So I asked the Holy Spirit to give me wisdom. The two ideas that came to me were to visit her and to bring her books to read.

I chose spiritual books that I thought might encourage her on her journey, especially during this fearful time of uncertainty in her pregnancy. During my visits we'd dialogue about what she was reading and how it related to her situation.

Finally, Naomi was released from the hospital but needed to stay on bed rest at home. I tried to work from home when her husband had to be at work. That way, if there was any emergency, I was available to drive her to the hospital.

One afternoon, I felt the Holy Spirit heavily impress on my heart the same psalm He had given me for other women I had interacted with over the years—Psalm 139. I knew He wanted me to take my Bible and read it to Naomi, to show her that God knew this baby in her womb and that He knew all the days He had planned for this precious one. I felt nervous walking down the stairs to her condo, but I proceeded to the front door, took a deep breath and knocked.

Her mother, Mary, opened the door, and with a smile and nod she welcomed me in. As I sat next to Naomi's bed, I knew the Holy Spirit was prodding me to open my Bible and share the psalm, but I chose not to. I don't know if it was fear or just plain laziness, but I knew I was disobeying the voice of God during my time with her.

Ignoring His Voice

When I left, a great sadness came over me. I felt so heavy that it was hard to climb the flight of stairs back to my condo. As soon as I walked inside, my roommate asked, "How'd it go?" I knew I couldn't add lying to my already heavy heart, so I shared with her my disobedience in not obeying the voice of the Holy Spirit to read Psalm 139 to Naomi.

My roommate, full of grace, kindly said, "Well, obey His voice next time. There will be a next time if you pray for it." I resolved then and there that the next time I went to visit Naomi, if the Holy Spirit prompted me, I would share the psalm with her.

I took time the next morning to pray, write in my journal and seek the Lord on why I didn't obey Him. It became clear to me that I felt that the risk of rejection from my neighbors was greater than from a stranger. I didn't want to take that risk and then have it destroy our relationship. My fears were: What if reading the psalm insulted her? What if the chapter felt trite to her situation? What if her husband, who was of a different faith, was present? After listing these fears, I decided I did not want "what ifs" to dictate my life or hinder me from obeying the voice of the Lord. I repented and asked the Lord to give me another opportunity to share this psalm with Naomi.

A Second Chance

Two days later, I went to visit Naomi again. This time, Alex was home, and he kept coming in and out of the bedroom as Joel, who was now one-and-a-half years old, was trying to walk alongside of the furniture. It was quite the distracting environment. Not quite the personal environment we had before. Yet, again, the Holy Spirit prodded me to ask her permission to read Psalm 139 to her. I took a deep breath and prayed, "Lord, I will obey You. Please give me courage to push through my fear." I then smiled and said to Naomi, "I was reading the Bible the other day and this chapter made me think of you and your pregnancy. I thought it might encourage you. May I read it to you?"

"Sure, of course."

"Let's look at it together," I said. I opened my Bible next to her on the bed and proceeded to read Psalm 139 out loud to her, stopping to explain the verses: He created her baby within her. He has every day planned for both her and the baby. He can hem her in behind and in front for protection. He loves them both.

As we were reading the psalm, Alex came into the room but didn't seem to notice or mind us reading the Bible out loud together. After I finished reading, I felt like the Holy Spirit wanted me to offer to pray for her. She was hurting physically, scared emotionally and hungry for spiritual comfort. Again she said, "Sure, of course!"

I prayed for her health, the baby's health, for God to comfort her and to reveal Himself to her during this challenging time. When I ended the prayer, Naomi had tears in her eyes and said, "No one's ever prayed for me before. Thank you so much. That was so special to me."

I had not thought about how some people have never been prayed over and how special that can be when it happens. It's something we do often in the Christian community, but we forget the impact and the encouragement it can be to those who do not yet know Jesus closely.

I left her home that day thanking God for a second chance to share that Scripture with her and pray over her. I thought about how I would have missed out on blessing her if I hadn't gone back with the intent of obeying the voice of the Holy Spirit.

Postpartum Depression

Due to the difficult pregnancy, Naomi had to have a C-section. This meant that we knew the day her second child would be born. I made it a point to take the time off work so that I could be there the hour Dana was born. It was an incredible honor to be with her family and celebrate this fragile life that was safely brought into the world.

About a year after Dana's birth, postpartum depression engulfed Naomi. As I was passing by their front door, heading home late one night, Alex flung the door open. Without even saying hi, he started to talk to me in a panicked voice. I stopped to focus on what he was trying to communicate about his wife.

"Naomi locked herself in the bathroom and wouldn't let me in! She drank toilet bowel cleaner and is crying hysterically!"

I tried to wrap my mind around what he was telling me. I couldn't picture Naomi locking herself in a bathroom and poisoning herself. It just didn't make sense.

Alex frantically continued, "Just five minutes ago, she opened the bathroom door and came out. I've been trying to convince her to go to the emergency room, but she doesn't want to. Maybe she will listen to you. Come in! Come in!"

I rushed into their living room at 11:30 at night. Naomi slowly walked out of the bathroom to meet us, definitely out of sorts. She'd clearly been crying.

Immediately, I went to hug her and enquired, "What's wrong? What happened, Naomi? Sit down and talk to me."

As she sat by me on the couch, she said, "I was hearing voices. They were telling me that I wasn't a good mother and that I should kill myself."

Alex starting lifting his voice, exclaiming, "If you died, it would leave our two children without a mother! Why would you try to do something like this to yourself? Don't you love me? Don't you love our children?"

Naomi was crying as I tried to reason with Alex. "Let's focus on getting her the help she needs right now; we can talk about the whys later. Is that okay?" He nodded and went to go check on his children in the other room.

I tried to talk slowly and calmly with Naomi. "We are so thankful you opened the bathroom door and told us you drank this cleaner. Naomi, you are a wonderful mother. God gave you these two children, and He will help give you wisdom how to raise them. The voices you heard in your head were not good or right. Alex loves you. Your children love you. I love you. We want you to be okay. I need to call poison control right now and get their advice on what assistance you might need."

Naomi kept insisting that she'd be fine, but I called the poison control hotline anyway. They said that the cleaner she'd consumed would increasingly swell her throat and stomach. It was necessary to take her to the emergency room as soon as possible. She was already admitting that she was having a hard time swallowing, which finally convinced her to go to the hospital. On the way there, sitting behind Alex and Naomi in the backseat, I prayed for God to keep her safe, heal her body and that the children wouldn't be traumatized by seeing their mother in that state.

Naomi was rushed in as soon as we arrived. About half an hour later, Alex came out and said they had pumped her stomach and had flushed out the poison. She was now stable but needed to stay a few more hours to take some psych tests. Since it was so late, he wanted to take me home and not have me wait.

On the way home, I asked Alex if he believed in evil forces, like demons. He said yes. I said, "I think we need to pray for Naomi. If voices were telling her she wasn't a good mom and were encouraging her to take her life, we need to pray that God protects her."

Alex nodded and said, "She had previously been diagnosed with postpartum depression but had stopped taking her pills. This might be the cause of the voices. But prayer is good."

Feelings of Shame

A few days later, I asked the Holy Spirit to fill me with wisdom as I went to visit Naomi for the first time since she returned home from the hospital. As we sat on the couch, fresh tears filled Naomi's eyes as she said, "I can't believe I tried to take my own life when I have two small children! I felt like I was going crazy!"

I asked her what she was feeling now. She replied, "Shame. I feel so ashamed."

It seemed like the depth of her shame was wearing her down. She needed hope. That's when the Holy Spirit brought to my mind this truth to declare to Naomi: "Jesus took upon Himself our shame while on the cross. He not only forgives us for the shameful things we have done, but He also takes our shame and puts it on Himself so that we don't have to bear the burden of it anymore. When you cry out to Jesus, He will forgive you, comfort you and help you to have a new peace and hope toward the future."

Naomi listened and nodded. She wasn't at a point yet to put her full trust and faith in Jesus, but she let me pray over her, asking Jesus to make His presence real to her so that she could find hope and joy again as she pressed on in life.

Facebook Message

This past week was my birthday, and of the many Facebook messages I received wishing me a happy birthday, the message from Naomi was the sweetest one of all. She had written on her wall: "Today is a very special day, 12/12/12. But it's even more special because it's the birthday of a very special person. Happy Birthday, dear friend, Holly Melton. We wish you a very wonderful day. Thank you for being such a wonderful friend, neighbor and when I needed most—my angel. Love ya. Xoxo."

Though Alex and Naomi might not know Jesus personally yet, they know one of His followers. I truly believe that bringing Jesus into our conversations has made us closer, and continuing the dialogue about Jesus will one day transform their lives in a powerful way.

MOMENT OF REFLECTION

When the Holy Spirit has come upon you . . .
you will be my witnesses in Jerusalem, and in Judea
and Samaria, and to the end of the earth.

ACTS 1:8

The journey to becoming a loving neighbor means taking the time to celebrate with them exciting events in their lives, whether it's a new job or a new birth. It also means taking the time to walk through the trials and crises that will come along their path. In order to reach our Jerusalem, we are called to listen to our neighbors, learn about them, love them and lead them to Jesus when an opportunity presents itself. The Holy Spirit wants to show us how we can build these relationships and engage in spiritual conversations.

- *Get to know your neighbors by asking more of their story, their background.* We might not all be good question askers, but the Holy Spirit can show us what to ask so that we learn about their culture, their interests, their jobs and their children (see Jas. 1:5).

- *Celebrate with them: new jobs, birthdays, milestones and holidays.* Ask the Holy Spirit what would bless them: a card, flowers, gift certificate? (See Rom. 12:15.)

- *Ask the Holy Spirit to give you the questions to learn about their spiritual background.* Continue to ask the Spirit to show you opportunities to share your ongoing journey with Jesus (see Acts 20:28).

- *See if the Holy Spirit wants you to invite them to an event that your church is hosting.*

- *Hang out with them outside of where you live to deepen the friendship over time.*

- *Ask the Holy Spirit to show you if you are to write them a note of encouragement, read Scripture with them or ask if you can pray with them* (see 1 Thess. 5:11).

- *If you ignored the prodding of the Holy Spirit in a specific circumstance, repent, receive His forgiveness and then be willing to go and obey that prodding the next opportunity you have* (see John 10:3,4,16,27).

Questions to Ponder

1. Who are your neighbors? Do you know their names? What they do? What are their backgrounds? Their spiritual journeys?

2. What is the next step the Spirit is placing on your heart to get to know your neighbors better?

Holly A. Melton

3. What are some of your fears in beginning a conversation about spiritual things? What might be challenging about bringing up Jesus in a conversation? How can you have courage to still take steps of faith despite those fears?

4. What is something you can invite your neighbors to attend with you?

Conversation with God

1. Ask the Holy Spirit to give you the courage to initiate getting to know your neighbors.

2. Admit your fears to Him and ask Him to conquer them as you choose to take steps of faith as the Spirit guides you.

3. Confess where you have ignored the prodding of the Holy Spirit and ask for another opportunity to obey and follow His lead.

4. Ask the Holy Spirit to give you the questions to ask, the words to say and the wisdom to know how to bring up spiritual things.

5. Ask the Holy Spirit to work in your neighbors' lives. Pray for them often.

Chapter 9

Professors, Billionaires and a Blue Dress

It's not every day that you go on a wild ride with the Holy Spirit, but when it happens, it's pretty incredible! That's what happened on my last day of class while I was on a summer's mission trip in the Middle East.

Eleven of us were taking a three-week class on politics at one of the most prominent universities in the Middle East. It was known to be the place where diplomats, presidents and kings sent their children to school. Our desire was to engage with the future leaders of the Middle East while we attended class there.

Our professor was quite distinguished. She was tenured, she was an author of two books on politics in the Middle East, and she had taught at Princeton and Oxford. It was an honor to be under her tutelage even for such a short time.

To be completely honest, as we headed into this summer, I wondered if our group could really make an impact in a Muslim country in just three weeks. What could possibly happen in such a short amount of time?

I learned that the answer is—a lot.

During the second week of school, we walked to class and found a note on the door informing us that our professor was not able to come to class that day. She had been in a car accident. The note said that she was fine and would be in class the next day.

Sure enough, our professor was in class the next day. She seemed more than a little dazed. She kept holding her stomach, but she taught the class, nonetheless. Afterward, I went up to her with one of the other students and said, "Professor Mohammad, I'm sorry to hear that you were in a car accident. We prayed for you when we heard about it. Are you all right?"

She smiled, nodded and said, "After the accident, the paramedics had a doctor check me out. He said that my baby will be fine."

I had no clue what she was talking about at first. Then I realized she was sharing with me that she was pregnant.

I laughed and said, "What? I didn't even know you were pregnant! I'm so glad to hear the baby is doing okay after that. I will continue to pray for you and your baby. I've really enjoyed your class, Professor Mohammad. I'm learning so much!"

Looking at me a bit surprised, she said, "Really? You think I'm a good teacher? But you're auditing!"

I smiled and said, "Just because I'm auditing doesn't mean I don't want to learn. I have learned so much under you."

I think that since I wasn't taking the class for a grade, she believed me; I wasn't kissing up to her.

Pensive for a moment, she looked at me and said, "I've lost two other babies. I was afraid I was going to lose this one too."

I realized she was sharing something extremely personal with me as she embraced me in a firm hug and said, "Thank you for asking."

All I had done was go up to her after class to ask how she was doing. I shared that I had prayed for her and expressed that I enjoyed her class. Those small steps seemed to open her up to me in ways I hadn't anticipated or even looked for.

The Letter

That night, like every other night, I was graciously awakened at 3:30 in the morning by the loud call to prayer blaring outside of my bedroom window. Usually, I'd just wake up briefly and then the chanting would lull me back to sleep. This night was different.

I felt impressed in my spirit to pray for my professor, her unborn child and her daughter, whom she had taken to the airport to fly to see her father. As I was praying, the Holy Spirit nudged me to write her a letter.

My first thought was, *Is it safe to write her a letter with spiritual undertones? Would she wonder what our group was doing here? Would it blow our cover?*

Whether it was safe or not, I knew I was being asked to write it, so I did.

Dear Dr. Mohammad,

Talking to you after class on Monday was very significant to me. One of my highest values is vulnerable communication, and for whatever reason, you chose to be vulnerable with me. It was my most precious, sacred moment so far in this country. Connecting with a person at a heart level about real life, feelings, trials, challenges, fears and failures means the world to me.

I am so glad you shared with me that you are pregnant and that your baby is fine after the accident. I saw you holding your stomach during class and I wondered if you weren't feeling well. I am sure the car accident was scary, especially in light of your previous miscarriages. Though I am not a mother and have not experienced the physical and emotional pain of losing a child, my heart broke for you and the challenges you have had to face.

You are a very successful woman. You have accomplished already so much in your lifetime. I feel privileged to be taking your class at such a significant time in this country's history. You have taught me so much already. However, I also know that you are not just a professor. You are a woman with a life journey, a life story, filled with joys and pain.

I learned after class that you just sent your daughter to America to visit her father there. That must be so hard and heartbreaking. I am sure there will be a great void in your heart while she is gone.

Last night, the call to prayer graciously woke me up at 3:30 AM. Unlike previous nights, where the call to prayer wakes me up only to sing me back to sleep again, I felt drawn to pray for you.

I know very little about you, and I have no clue as to what your religious beliefs or practices are. But I felt impressed upon my heart to pray for you, your baby and your daughter heading to America. As I prayed for peace, comfort and safety, a poem came to my mind that is one I treasure. The prophet David wrote it, and it is found in Psalm 139 in the holy Bible.

My theory, as I've traveled around the world, is that we humans have two great desires: to be fully known (all of our good and all of our bad) and still be fully loved. I guess I've become skeptical that this could be found on this side of heaven. I truly believe, though, where man may fail us, God won't. That is why I often cling to this psalm when I wonder, "Why was I born? Does God see me? Know me? Does He care? Does He have a plan for my life?" I have come to believe that He does. This poem reminds me of that often.

May it, too, bring you encouragement. He formed you. You are fearfully and wonderfully made. His thoughts toward you far outnumber the sand (and there's lots of sand in the Middle East!). May it comfort you to know that your two other babies are with their loving Creator. They are safe in His arms.

Maybe meeting you is the reason I came to the Middle East. Only God knows, but I am glad to have met you, learn from you, and to have gotten a small glimpse into your life.

Prayers and blessings, Holly

The next day after class, I anxiously waited for Professor Mohammad to come out of the room to hand her the letter. She seemed surprised to receive it, so I told her she could read it later.

The following day she came up to me in the hallway and said, "Thank you so much for your letter. It was the nicest letter I've ever received from a student. It made me cry."

We hugged, and I said, "I'm glad to hear that it blessed you!"

Crisis in Class

It was our last day of class and we were giving final presentations. During one of the students' presentations, Professor Mohammad interrupted her. She wanted the student to change the direction of her presentation because she felt like the student was being too biased toward one point of view.

A fellow student watching the presentation immediately jumped up to defend the other student. Unheard of behavior in this culture, this male student and Professor Mohammad began arguing, heatedly, in each other's face. Finally, the professor told him she would not continue class unless he left. He said he wouldn't leave the room until he had given his presentation. At a standstill, our professor turned around, silently walked to the back of the room and picked up her books. She walked toward the door.

The room was dead quiet. No one moved. As the door closed behind her, I saw her crumple over, as if someone had punched her in the stomach. I got up and ran out the door to her. When she removed her right hand from her black skirt, I saw that it was bloody.

She looked up at me from her hunched-over position and cried out, "I'm losing my baby! I'm losing my baby!"

I was shocked to see the blood. I wasn't sure what to do in that situation. I tried to walk her to the bathroom, but she could barely walk. I partially carried her down the hall.

Two more students came out of the classroom to see what was happening. Professor Mohammad's demeanor instantly changed. She looked at the three of us and shouted, "Get the f— away! Get the f— away!"

Sobbing, she hobbled into the bathroom alone.

Stunned, the three of us just waited outside, discussing what to do next.

About a minute later, our professor came out. Her hands were clean, but mascara tears stained her face. She shouted, "Back to class. We must finish the presentations."

I had no clue how she would go about concentrating on three more presentations, but we all went back and sat down in our seats to try to re-engage. I couldn't. I just sat there.

I began to pray fervently: *Oh, Holy Spirit, please give me wisdom. Should I approach our professor after class? What can I do? Please make me safe so that she'll open up to me. Give me the opportunity to talk to her alone after class. Oh, Holy Spirit, I need wisdom. Help me to know what to do and say. Please, Holy Spirit, open her heart to talk to me. Please.*

I just prayed and prayed and prayed and prayed.

Kaitlyn, a girl on our team, gave the last presentation. She spoke about women who have influenced politics in this country over the years. They each had three characteristics in common: They were strong, they persevered and they were persecuted. That was the only part of her presentation I heard. I wrote those words down in my notes and kept praying.

At the end of class, our professor apologized for her behavior with the other student. She said she didn't want to end on that note, so she'd like to have the class over for a party in a few days. Then she picked up her things and started to head out of the classroom. It was the most intense, crazy day we had in class all summer.

After Class

The day wasn't over yet. When Professor Mohammad walked out, I felt this pull on my heart. I knew that I needed to follow her. The worst she could do was keep walking and tell me to "get the f— away" again. So, I followed her.

She looked back, saw me and slowed down. I walked faster. Down the hallway was a pillar. She walked over to it and stood behind it, seeming to be waiting for me.

As I reached her side, she immediately broke down into heaving sobs and said with fear and trembling, "I'm losing my baby! I'm losing my baby! I was so mean to that kid! I should never have been that mean! I'm losing my baby! I can't do this alone! Why was I so mean? I should lose my job!"

Back and forth, she was trying to process all that happened in the last hour. It was all too overwhelming for her. I suggested I help walk her back to her classroom. Instead, she looked up at me and said, "Will you come home with me? My driver can take you home afterward. I can't do this alone. I can't let my husband know. He doesn't even know that I am pregnant. Please come home with me. Please. I can't do this. I just can't."

All of me wanted to help her, but what was going through my mind was, *We aren't allowed to go places alone. It's not safe. I can't go with her. I don't even have a way to talk to my co-leader to make this decision.* I said I'd walk her to her car.

On the way to the parking lot, she fell against the wall, clearly in a lot of pain. She looked at me and said, "Why do I trust you? Why do I feel like you need to be with me right now? You are just a student."

I must admit, with my Sesame Street T-shirt, cargo capris and flip-flops, I did look like a younger student.

At this point, I had a strong feeling that I should call her by her first name. All of my cultural training went out the window, because technically, it is more honoring to call her "Professor" since she worked so hard to gain that title. Yet, I couldn't shake the feeling that I was to call her by her first name, Mable.

I took a deep breath, put my hand on her trembling shoulder and said, "Mable, you don't understand. First of all, today was our last day of class, so technically I am no longer your student. Second, I am 34 years old. I'm not your typical college student."

She looked at me in unbelief and said, "No way! You seem like you are only 24! I don't believe it. You can't be!"

I finally convinced her of my age, and we proceeded to walk toward her car.

As we were walking, those three words from the final presentation, describing women who have strived for success in a Muslim culture, came to mind. I looked at Mable and said, "I believe what Kaitlyn shared in class about women needing to be strong, persevering and yet sadly persecuted in this culture is what you seem to have survived to become a professor. I see you as a strong woman. You've written books. You've taught at elite schools all over the Western world. You've persevered through many obstacles to be a successful woman in the Middle East. I am sure you've been persecuted along the way."

She looked at me with her mouth gaping open and said, "How did you know? That's exactly what it's been like for me! Did you know that no one in this school likes me? They probably would all try to get me fired, but I'm tenured, so they can't. I have no friends, no community."

At that point we were at the door to her car. As her driver held open the door, she motioned to me and said, "Get in!" as if she were impatiently waiting for me to join her.

So I took another deep breath, wondering what I was doing, and got in.

And Then It Got Awkward

Being a rule follower, I knew that I was breaking the rules by driving away, alone, with Mable. Yet, I felt that the Holy Spirit wanted me to go with her. She was opening up to me, and for some reason, I knew that this was not normal for her. God was up to something, and I wanted to be a part of it.

Inside the car, I texted my co-leader so that he would at least know where I was going and what was happening. Then I placed my attention back on Mable. I continued to listen as she kept volleying back and forth between the fear of having another miscarriage and the humiliation of how she had treated the student in the class.

After letting her talk it out, I asked, "Mable, can you give yourself grace right now? The young man will be okay. You can revisit the conflict with him in class another day. We just need to get you home and have you focus on taking care of yourself and your baby right now."

As we continued to talk, it was as if something switched inside of her. Her eyes grew wide and round with great anxiety, and she sputtered, "Oh, my goodness! I . . . I think I fancy you! I don't know . . . what to do! I have *never* felt this way about any man or woman before! It's like I want to jump you right now! Oh, my! I can't be a lesbian! I can't! You need to get out of my car *right* now!"

I froze in shock as I was trying to comprehend what was happening. I was not ready for her to freak out on me again. I thought we had established some trust in the past hour, but now, apparently, she was feeling emotions she wasn't sure how to handle. I prayed a quick prayer as I looked outside the car window. I knew it wouldn't be safe for me to be dropped off on the side of the road. The streets were filled mainly with men. I had no context to know where I was, and there were no apparent taxis in sight.

Through the Holy Spirit, I calmly looked at Mable and said, "You are not going to drop me off on the side of the road. We are taking you home so that you can rest. If you want your driver to take me home at that point, that's fine, but I'm not leaving this car while you are in this state."

She looked at me in confusion and replied, "But why am I feeling this way? This is freaking me out!"

I looked at her and again spoke calmly. "For the past 45 minutes, I have been engaging with you on a deep emotional level. You shared things with me that your own husband doesn't even know. That trust and vulnerability create what is called emotional intimacy. That is what usually helps women to be attracted to others. In our case, you may have never felt as known or accepted as you have in this past hour. It's a lot to sift through and process."

A noticeable peace settled over her when she heard my explanation. She said, "Holly, you are wise for your years."

Smiling I said, "I just know that people want to be fully known and fully loved—including you. God created the intimacy you are experiencing with me. God was the one that had you open up to me after class the day after your accident. God was the one who woke me up with the call to prayer at 3:30 in the morning to write you a letter. God was the one who blessed you by reading it. God was the one who encouraged you to reach out and ask for my help while you were bleeding outside of our class today. This has all been orchestrated by God."

This seemed to calm her, and soon we arrived at her house.

An Unexpected Phone Call

When I walked into her home, I was amazed at how clean, modern and American her décor was. Eyeing the beautifully painted walls, tiled kitchen, plush living room furniture and hardwood floors, I felt right at home.

She headed to her seven-year-old daughter's bedroom so that she could lie on the bed in an air-conditioned room. I followed her. As she curled up in a fetal position, she motioned to me and said, "Come sit by me."

I just stood there. I wasn't sure if it was wise to sit by her on the bed in her vulnerable emotional state, especially after what she had expressed on the car ride over.

Grasping my hesitancy, she said, "Don't worry. I'm not going to do anything to you. I just need to be comforted."

I'm not the type of girl that likes to cuddle with women, play with their hair or even link arms; but I took another step of faith and sat by her on the bed. She snuggled in. I quickly asked the Lord how to handle this situation. It was clear that I needed to begin to pray for her out loud. I didn't ask her if I could pray for her. I just stated that I was going to pray and dove in.

"Lord, I pray for Mable right now. She's in a lot of pain, and she's afraid. Lord, we pray for her baby right now. Please stop the bleeding and protect her baby. We know from Psalm 139 that You created this baby in a secret place. You have all the days planned for her. Lord, You love Mable. Please show her Your love."

At that moment, Mable started crying and shaking her head, saying, "No! No! God cannot love me! I am not a good person. It's not possible!"

I patted her head. Once again, I felt the role reversal in our relationship, as well as her desperate need for the Lord to reveal Himself to her. I said, "Mable, you are wrong. God does love you. Despite what you've ever done, He loves you. Despite how you see yourself, He sees you differently."

Just then her cell phone rang and she asked me to go get it. When she answered it, it was her husband, Shady. Her demeanor wasn't getting any happier as they talked. Finally, she said, "Shady, I had a really challenging day in class with one of my students. It was so draining that I am now an emotional wreck. One of my other students came home with me and is here right now. I do not feel well enough to go out tonight . . ."

She put her hand over the phone and whispered to me, "Would you please talk to my husband and explain to him what happened today? But don't tell him that I am having a miscarriage. He doesn't even know that I am pregnant."

Before I could even shake my head no, she handed me the phone. I was talking to Shady, her husband, whom I had never met. His English was practically flawless, and he seemed very caring and nice.

When I tried to think of a diplomatic way to explain the day's events, Shady said, "I am so glad you came home with Mable. It makes me feel so much better knowing that you are with her since I can't be there right now. Would you please stay with her until I come home?"

I said that would be fine and then handed the phone back to Mable.

When she got off of the phone, she explained to me that he was at his business partner's house for a dinner party. He had wanted her to come. She was thankful that I talked to him and that he seemed okay that she wasn't going to join him.

After she'd changed into more comfortable clothes and settled in on the living room couch, her phone rang again. It was Shady. He said that he really did need her to be there. She needed to get dressed immediately and come to this dinner party. She looked so drained, still in pain, but she said she would get ready and join him.

The Blue Dress

When she got off the phone she looked at me and said, "We're going to a party. Come on. We have to get ready!"

My brain started spinning a mile a minute. I'm not supposed to be alone in this country, and now I am getting invited to a party!

I looked at her and gave her the only meager excuse I could conjure up. "I'm wearing a Sesame Street T-shirt. I don't think I am dressed for a dinner party."

She smiled and gave me a look implying that I was being silly and said, "Holly, I have a whole wardrobe of clothes. I know exactly what you're going to wear tonight too."

Getting up slowly, she walked to her bedroom closet. She pulled out a slinky, light blue, shimmery dress. This is not the sort of dress I would wear in America, let alone in a conservative Muslim country! However, she didn't offer me any other options, so I put it on.

Next thing I knew, she was whisking me out of the house to her car. Her driver was waiting for us, once again. I got into the car and texted my co-leader, Jon, to let him know what I was doing. Each moment of this crazy adventure felt like a risk. I was praying through each step of it, and all I knew was that I needed to stay with my professor. As we started to drive, Mable explained that we weren't just going to any house; we were going to a billionaire's house—the tenth richest man in the nation. Mable's husband was the manager of one of his five companies. No wonder they were so well off.

When we entered the neighborhood, it looked like a version of the mansions in Hollywood; yet this was even grander! We arrived at the mansion and walked over cement lily pads that were surrounded by water to get to the front door. The home was unique, with detailed architecture. The landscaping contained multiple fountains, specially imported trees and lush green grass—all of this in the middle of the desert!

After Mable rang the doorbell twice, a voice spoke through the outside intercom, asking who we were. Mable explained who she was. Then the 10-foot-high copper door opened to reveal the billionaire's wife. Olive-skinned, dyed blonde hair and appearing to be quite anorexic, she extended her bejeweled hand, welcoming us into her home. I thanked her for letting me join my professor for the evening.

The living room in front of us held an infinity pool near the glass wall. You could go swimming in their living room. Everything—paintings, sculptures and furniture—was exquisite. Each item seemed to have been imported from all over the world.

Kissed by a Billionaire

I noticed immediately that there was no one else in the house. The dining room table was set for an intimate dinner, but where were the guests? The billionaire's wife ushered us toward the backyard where there was an outdoor living space of plush couches, pillows and surround-sound TV. I met her husband, Mr. Billionaire, and he kissed me on both cheeks. Apparently, that is the custom in this culture. It was the one time that summer I wished I had Internet so I could put on my Facebook status, "I was just kissed *twice* by a billionaire!"

Mable introduced me to her husband, Shady. He again thanked me for coming home with her since she'd had such a difficult day.

I looked around and realized that there were only two other men there. As I was introduced, I quickly learned that I was meeting the CEO of a large French car company and his business partner. They were in the country for just two days, specifically to make a deal with Mr. Billionaire about bringing their cars into the country. This was a private dinner party. I was the odd woman out, making the total dinner guests seven.

My head began to swirl with questions. *What in the world was I doing there? How did I end up in this situation? How am I to interact with these elite people?*

I usually joke with my friends and say that I prefer not to network in my job, and that small talk is not my cup of tea. I prefer engaging in deeper conversation to really get to know a person. I like to be intentional. That caused me to ponder, *Why am I in this crazy, unusual situation?*

The only reason I could conjure up was that I was to be a support for my professor. All evening, through hors d'oeuvres, wine, cheese and intriguing (though slightly pointless) conversation, Mable kept coming up to me. She would hug me, say that she loved me and was so thankful I was there with her.

We had the most delicious dinner of my entire summer, with lively conversation about politics in the country. After dessert and coffee, my unusual night came to a close as Mable and Shady accompanied me to my home with their driver.

I learned a few days later that after dropping me off at my home that night, Mable lost her baby. When she told me this in a flat, emotionless voice, she stretched out her fingers and said, "My child was about two inches long."

She started to tear up, finally feeling some emotion, but quickly pushed it away. She couldn't talk about it. She tried to change the subject by mentioning that she wanted to have me over again before I left the country. She wanted me to come over on Saturday night.

I wrestled with whether it was wise to go to her place again, alone. If her husband wasn't home, and I was alone with her, would she try to come on to me? Would I be safe if her driver picked me up and dropped me off at my home alone?

My co-leader, Jon, and I talked it over. We took time to pray about it. Both of us agreed that I might be setting myself up for an uncomfortable situation if Mable did make any advances. Yet it seemed to be worth the risk if it was my only opportunity to share the gospel with her before I left.

So, in faith and much prayer, I had her driver pick me up and take me to her house.

Talking About Vampires and Other Spiritual Things

As soon as I entered her home, Mable began making us a snack in the kitchen. As I was helping her cut up some vegetables, she said, "You know, I'm not getting any younger. I've been thinking a lot about what will happen when I die. Will I go to heaven? Will there be enough room in heaven for everyone?"

I listened as she listed all of these questions she'd been pondering. I was amazed that she was the one bringing up spiritual issues, not me!

She then said, as if it were a side thought, "Huh. I never asked you what you do for a living!"

I had wondered if this question would ever come up. I was thankful that in the past year I had become a certified life coach. I explained, "I'm currently a life coach, but I would also like to be an author and speaker one day. Do you know what a life coach is?"

"Yes, I do. But in my opinion, the reason people hire a life coach is because the churches and mosques are not doing their jobs."

I couldn't have agreed with her more! I then explained how when I coach people, I use principles found in the Bible because there is practical advice there that can really guide our lives.

Mable then began to share more of her story. Her first husband (with whom she had her daughter) was Jewish. She asked, "What is the difference between Christians and Jews?"

I saw this as an opportunity to explain a little about Jesus.

"Really, the difference between Christians, Jews and even Muslims is their understanding of who Jesus was. Christians believe He was the Messiah that the Jews were waiting for. The Jews weren't convinced. They thought a Messiah would free them from physical oppression from the Romans, rather than spiritual oppression from sin. Muslims see Jesus as a prophet, which He was. However, He was the only perfect prophet, and that's significant. He was the only prophet who could adequately die in our place for our sins."

She looked at me, pondered what I had said, and then asked, "Weren't *all* of the prophets perfect?"

I smiled and said, "Nope! You know the prophet David, whom we call King David? Well, he committed adultery and then killed someone. Yet, he confessed his sin, still wanting to walk with God. He was a good man, but not perfect."

Intently listening, Mable replied, "Oh! I didn't know that. No one's ever explained this to me."

She then asked what I wanted to write about or speak on in the future. I told her that I wanted to write a book called *The Vampire Who Changed My Life*.

She looked at me, very intrigued, and said, "Really? Do tell! I love horror stories!"

I laughed a little and said, "Well, I don't know if it's really a horror story . . . but it certainly has a good ending!"

The next half hour I proceeded to tell her the story of Christy the vampire. I made sure to clearly share the gospel. I explained how Jesus was relevant even to a woman who thought she was a vampire.

Mable hung on my every word.

At the end of the story, she looked at me with big eyes and said, "I have never heard of someone's life changing like that! That was incredible! Holly, I believe God has great purpose for you in this world."

I once again had to laugh inside at how our God works. Who would have thought 13 years after Christy the vampire became a follower of Jesus, I would be able to share her story with a Muslim in the Middle East so that she could hear the gospel. Sometimes God's strategies just make me smile and laugh.

As we stood by her wall of windows, looking out at the city lights, I said, "Mable, there's one thing I believe God does with me. He enables people to trust me who usually have a hard time trusting people. Christy had a very hard time trusting anyone. And you admitted the other day that you, too, have no real friends. You haven't even been able to tell your husband that you were pregnant or had a miscarriage, yet you trusted me. I was a stranger who popped into your life for just three short weeks as a student in your class. You had no reason to trust me. No reason to share with me your life, your pain. No reason to invite me to your house, or to the billionaire's house, for that matter. But you did! I believe that God enables people to trust me *so that* I can share Jesus with them."

Mable listened and nodded.

I continued, "I truly believe you were the reason I came to the Middle East this summer. God wanted to unite us in the midst of this time of tragedy in your life so that I could befriend you and tell you about Jesus."

Just then the door opened, and Shady walked in. Perfect timing. God's timing, which as always, is perfect.

The Gifts

The three of us hung out for about an hour longer. Mable even asked me to share the "vampire story" with Shady. I felt like it wasn't the right time, though, and suggested that she share it with him the next day. I learned later that she did.

As we were talking, my phone rang. It was Jon. I hadn't realized how much time had passed—it was already 11:30 at night. It was time for me to say good-bye.

I had brought gifts for Mable but had wanted her to open them without Shady around. That didn't seem possible anymore, so I handed her the gifts and whispered, "Wait until I call you from the car, and then you can open them."

We hugged good-bye. She said she loved me, would miss me tons and their family would plan to come visit me in California someday.

As her chauffeur was driving me away in her car, I called her. I told her to open the bigger gift first. It was a New Testament in both Arabic and English. I encouraged her to read it so that she could learn more about Jesus.

She said thank you and that she would most definitely read it.

Then, I asked her to open the smaller gift. It was a silver ring with four rubies in it. I told her that I had no clue if this ring was going to fit her, but it had a special meaning.

"There are four rubies on this ring. From now on, I want you to remember that you are a mom of four children, not a mom of one. Three of your children are in the loving arms of God. One has been entrusted into your loving arms to care for until, I pray, one day we are all united with Jesus in heaven."

Mable was quiet for a moment. Then she said, "Thank you, Holly. This means so much to me. I love you so much."

With tears in my eyes, I told her that we'd keep in contact and that I loved her too.

The clock struck midnight near the end of the phone call. I sat alone in the backseat of her car, and I couldn't help but believe that God wasn't finished with Professor Mohammad. He didn't bring me to the other side of the world to experience such a crazy situation and not have Him impact her life. Tears started to stream down my face. Thankful for the darkness of the car, I turned on my iPod to listen to worship music the rest of the way home. As I thought about the last few days, I was humbled to grasp that the Lord chose to use me with this person, in this country, for such a time as this.

Email from the Middle East

I left the country not knowing if I'd ever hear from Mable again. To my joy and surprise, she wrote me back a few months after my return to the states.

My Dearest Holly,

I am so sorry I have not contacted you earlier. I got really sick after you left and had a serious fever for about 5-6 days. I really thought the end had come! Truly!

Thanks for the pictures. I will print one and frame it in our home now that life is settling down.

We will certainly visit you soon. I hope you are now staying focused on your book, because you have a very special story and it MUST be told.

I will write again soon. We miss you!

You are simply a very special person. Remember that.

Lots of love,

Mable, Shady and Kimber xxxx

P.S. Your ring is very special to me. I wear it all the time.

We don't always know what impact we leave in our wake. I continually pray that my wake will leave waves in the souls of others until they cry out to Jesus to save them from the storms of their lives.

MOMENT OF REFLECTION

But when the Helper comes, whom I will send to you from the Father, the Spirit of truth, who proceeds from the Father, he will bear witness about me. And you also will bear witness, because you have been with me from the beginning.

JOHN 15:26-27

This story, just like the vampire story, does not reflect what life is like every day for me. But these situations are a reminder that God wants to use us in the lives of people who live differently than we do. What if I thought there was no way I could come alongside my professor? What if I thought that because she is successful she must be doing fine, not experiencing any problems? What if I had just let her walk out of the classroom and didn't choose to take the initiative to go after her?

• *The Holy Spirit wants to use us to influence those who influence others.* We don't often consider how the Lord might want to have us enter in more deeply with those who are leading and guiding us. He might want us to risk talking about spiritual things with our family members, our professors or even our employers in the workplace. We can be too quick to say that we cannot talk about spiritual things in these contexts, and we miss some extraordinary opportunities. We need to push through the cultural norm that says, "Don't go too deep with those who lead you." Elijah needed Elisha when he was afraid and weary. Moses needed Aaron to help him speak to the people. David needed Nathan to speak truth to him when he was in sin. Leaders need followers to influence them at certain times in their lives. Leaders aren't islands, meant to live in isolation. Who else will reach out to them if not those of us walking in the power of the Holy Spirit?

• *The Holy Spirit is given to us to help us share truth with others* (see John 16:13). I had to respond to the nudge of the Holy Spirit at 3:30 in the morning when I felt impressed to write to my professor. That letter was my first step in sharing the truth of who God is, from Psalm 139. That step of faith seemed really intimidating and risky, but I was obeying that small voice of instruction that helped begin the journey with my professor. You, too, might need to respond to a nudge or a thought to initiate with someone who usually leads and influences you.

Holly A. Melton

- *The Holy Spirit will bear witness about Jesus* (see John 15:26; 1 John 5:6). I am no expert on Islam, nor do I feel confident on how to best share the gospel with Muslims. Yet the Holy Spirit didn't need me to have years of training to bring the gospel to my professor. He used a story from the past to bring the gospel into the present. The focus of our conversation was still Jesus: who people thought He was and why He came to earth and died. The Holy Spirit will help us keep the topic on Jesus. My role was not to try to convince her who Jesus is; that's the Holy Spirit's role. I just needed to be willing to talk about Him.

- *The Holy Spirit does not need us to be on the same level as those we are influencing.* We often hide behind excuses such as, "I'm not rich enough to talk to the wealthy"; "I don't have a high enough education to talk to those who are experts in their fields"; "I'm not pretty enough to reach the outwardly beautiful people." These comparisons and assumptions will hinder us from living an extraordinary life. We must remember that we have been given all authority, which was given to Jesus (see Matt. 28:18). We must remember that wealth, education and beauty do not negate people's need to hear about Jesus. If the Holy Spirit can use even a student in a Sesame Street T-shirt to bring the power of the gospel to an esteemed Muslim professor, how much more might He want to use you?

Questions to Ponder

1. Who are the influential people in your life that God might want you to get to know on a more personal level? How can you enter more into their world?

2. What fears do you have in taking the steps of faith to try to go deeper with these people?

3. What inklings have you had that maybe you should try to act on?

4. What are ways you can show your appreciation for the people you've identified as influential in your life?

Conversation with God

1. Ask the Holy Spirit which influencers in your life He might want you to pursue more personally.

2. Ask the Holy Spirit to give you "peace that passes all understanding" (see Phil. 4:7) as you renounce your fears and commit to taking a step of faith that He puts on your mind or heart.

3. Ask the Holy Spirit to use you to bring the truth of Jesus to others.

4. Ask the Holy Spirit to open up the mind and heart of the person you want to influence.

Part Two

Following His Lead

The Holy Spirit, the Spirit of truth (see John 15:26), wants us to follow His lead so that He can transform our lives and the lives of others. For many years, I thought this was only an optional following. I thought I could go to church, read the Bible and try to be a good person, and that was all I needed to do to walk with the Lord. It wasn't until I was in my early 20s that I started to learn about the role of the Holy Spirit in our lives. For the first time, I was able to see how the Holy Spirit gave me the power to overcome my sinful flesh and walk in true freedom.

It was also the first time I learned that I could actually pray to the Holy Spirit to guide me in my relationships with others and see how He would work through me. Grasping these two roles of the Spirit has not only transformed my life, but also the lives of many others around me.

I've come to believe that of all the commands in the Bible, there is one that, if obeyed, encompasses them all: "Be filled with the Spirit" (Eph. 5:18). Here's what happens when we follow His lead: We walk away from temptation and say no to sin (see 1 Cor. 10:13); we take steps of faith and gain courage where there was once fear; we forgive others and pursue restoration with them; we speak truth in love (see Eph. 4:15); we are able to live out the fruit of the Spirit: love, joy, peace, patience, kindness, goodness, faithfulness, gentleness and self-control (see Gal. 5:22-23); we are able to bring Jesus into our spiritual conversations with others; we share verses that touch the souls of men; we pray prayers that heal and encourage (see Jas. 5:16); we bless others in ways we had no idea would matter to them.

When we are filled with the Spirit, we become more like Jesus, and share Him with others.

No matter where you are in your walk with the Lord, you can see the Lord work through your life if you do one thing: walk in the power of the Holy Spirit by responding to His voice. If you learn what this means and live this out day by day, you will see divine interactions everywhere.

I ask myself one question over and over again every day: "Am I doing this in the power of the Holy Spirit or the Holly spirit?" Your name might not sound as cool in that question (or as corny), but the question is still the same. Are you living your life in your own strength or by the strength of the Spirit of God who is at work within you?

The next few chapters will discuss three ways you can practically follow His lead: (1) out of sin, (2) into service, and (3) through surrender. As you learn how to walk in the Spirit and not your flesh, you can then be more aware of the Spirit's guiding in your life to engage with others. And if you want to engage with others, you must consider living a surrendered life to Him. Only then will you see your life and the lives around you transformed by the power of the Holy Spirit.

Chapter 10

Follow His Lead
Out of Sin

We cannot expect the Holy Spirit to work powerfully through us to impact others' lives if we first don't allow Him to work powerfully in us toward our own sanctification. To be transformed, we must overcome habitual sin in our lives (see Rom. 12:2). This can happen when we learn how to walk in the power of the Holy Spirit. Sadly, it seems that few Christians have grasped this, so they live defeated lives. I saw this with my friend Shannon.

Letters of Confession

Shannon is a believer, but she struggled with alcohol. After admitting she needed help, she went to Christian rehab and, over time, celebrated years of being sober. It seemed as if her life was getting back on track and she was finding victory over the temptations in her life.

I decided to send her a personal Facebook message to ask how she was doing. Her reply reminded me of how quickly we can get engulfed in our sinful ways. Even when we've seen some victory in our life, even when we know what the Bible says about sin, our fleshly desires can overwhelm us until we give in to them when we don't know how to follow the leading of the Holy Spirit.

Here was her reply:

Dear Holly

How am I? Young and foolish about sums it up, I suppose. I think that will be the official title of this year of my life. Honestly, Holly—my life is leaps and bounds better than when I was drinking (speaking of which, I'm 2½ years sober now! Can you believe it?), but it's still awfully messy.

I'm in a relationship that I love, with a man I love, knowing full well that it's a far cry from God's best for me. (Two good indicators of that: he's ardently agnostic, and our relationship is sexual.) I'm 26 years old now, and I feel like I still haven't nearly figured out how to be an adult who has a real job, a decent place to live and who walks humbly with her God.

So please pray (gulp) that God would convict me about this relationship, because I can't even bring myself to pray that yet. To be brutally honest, I just like sex way too much to ask God to help me even want to give that up.

Thank you, Holly—I know your prayers are powerful. Shannon

My heart broke when I read Shannon's words. She was free of one addiction only to grab on to another. It's not like she didn't know this relationship wasn't God's best for her; she just wasn't able, in her own strength, to give it up. Three months later, she wrote to me again:

As for me . . . I don't have just one word to describe how I'm doing. How about "a beautiful mess"? Still with Ted, the guy I told you about, and . . . sigh . . . quite in love . . . with a guy who doesn't know the Lord . . . who I'm still in a sexual relationship with. And how the bleep did that happen, you ask? Beats the bleep out of me.

If I had known in college that this is where I would be at 27, I never would have believed it. I would have told you that I love the Lord way too much to let something like this happen (I also would

have told you that I love the Lord too much to become an alcoholic).
And yet . . . well, since the end of college, I seem to have stumbled
through one monstrous sin after the next.

I think one of the hardest parts is that it's SO difficult for me to
still believe that God's grace extends even to me, even to my sins. That
I can't out-sin it. I would tell someone else that in a heartbeat, but
when it comes to believing that truth in my own life, I fall short. So I
talk to God less, because I don't believe He really wants to hear from
me. And my life becomes more and more imbalanced and cold, and
I cling to things of this world for warmth, like a relationship that I'm
pretty bleeping sure isn't God's best for me. But it's SO big in my life
right now, because I've made God so small. Once again, you'd think
I'd have learned that lesson through alcoholism, right? Apparently
not. My head really is that hard.

Anyway, all that to say, I LOVE your prayers, I LOVE hearing
truth from you (even when it's hard), and I would love, love, LOVE
to see you in April! Shannon

How do you feel when you read this story? What do you think
is the disconnect in what Shannon knows about God and how she
is living? How did she get there? There are many people, like Shannon, who are stuck in habitual sin.

I so appreciate that Shannon was open and honest with me; unfortunately, just being honest and vulnerable won't stop habitual
sin from happening. Just admitting that you are sinning, though a
good first step, does not help you stop sinning.

We often think that if someone admits to us that he or she is in
sin, then he or she will feel convicted and stop; but sometimes it's
not that easy.

To see habitual sin purged out of our lives, we must have a right
view of God (He is both merciful and just) and a right view of ourselves
(we are sinners saved by grace). We must not only admit that we have
sinned, but we must also ask the Lord to grow our understanding of
the depth of our sin to lead us to repentance. When we come to a point
of remorse over our sin (not just feeling guilty), then we are ready to ask
the Spirit to come and start to change us from within.

Holly A. Melton

I do want to mention that some habitual sin behavior goes so deep that you need to find what the root of the behavior is. If you wrestle with deep anger or run frequently to addictions like pornography, alcohol, sex or obsessive eating, you may first need help discovering what is causing you to run to those things. If this is true in your situation, I would encourage you to get biblical counseling, join an AA program or read some of Neil Anderson's books on breaking strongholds (see 2 Cor. 10:4). His book *The Bondage Breaker* can be very helpful.

To truly become more like Jesus, there are seven questions we can ask ourselves to follow the Holy Spirit's lead out of the everyday sins we commit.

Seven Questions

These seven questions can simply be answered yes or no, but if you really take time to think about them, they are not easy to immediately say yes to. These questions are taken from studying the book of Galatians, chapter five. I'd encourage you to read this short chapter and ask the Holy Spirit to give you greater understanding and conviction before reading on.

Question 1:
Do you desire to live in freedom?

For freedom Christ has set us free; stand firm therefore, and do not submit again to a yoke of slavery.
GALATIANS 5:1

We are meant to have freedom after we decide to follow Jesus. Unfortunately, many people still feel like they live in bondage to the sin that so easily entangled them before they decided to follow Him. This is because they are trying to walk with Jesus in their own strength and not by the power offered them by the Spirit.

If you are like my friend Shannon, you may admit that you're not at a place where you want freedom from a certain sin. This is the first real question you must wrestle with: Do you want freedom?

- If you are unable to say yes to this question, be honest with the Lord. Admit that you enjoy your sin and are having a hard time giving it up.

- Ask Him to give you a desire to be free from it and to want to stand firm by the power of the Spirit that He provides. Your heart must get to a place where you *want* to live free from sin for the Spirit to work within you.

Question 2:
Do you desire to become more like Jesus?

For through the Spirit, by faith, we ourselves eagerly
wait for the hope of righteousness.
GALATIANS 5:5

We know that we will not be perfect this side of heaven. Even though we must wait until we are in heaven to be perfectly righteous, we can become more and more like Jesus as we daily walk with Him by His Spirit.

Some people are complacent with their lives. They don't want to become any more like Jesus before they get to heaven. We should be *eager* about seeing our lives continually change and become more holy and righteous now, this side of heaven. If this is not your desire, be honest with the Lord about your state of complacency. Ask yourself why you don't want to become more like Him.

The book of Revelation mentions the church in Laodicea, whose works were neither cold nor hot, but lukewarm. They were warned that if they stayed lukewarm in their relationship with the Lord, He would spit them out of His mouth. He warns, "For you say, I am rich, I have prospered, and I need nothing, not realizing that you are wretched, pitiable, poor, blind, and naked" (Rev. 3:17).

- Ask the Lord to reveal to you if you are complacent in parts of your life where you know there is sin or laziness.

- Ask Him to grow your desire to become more passionate in your walk with Him.

Question 3:
Are you willing to start focusing on others and not just on yourself?

For you were called to freedom, brothers. Only do not use your freedom as an opportunity for the flesh, but through love serve one another.
GALATIANS 5:13

Part of walking in the power of the Holy Spirit is taking our focus off of ourselves and putting it on caring and ministering to others. When we begin to love and serve others in the power of the Spirit, our flesh is no longer our focus, and we experience more joy and fulfillment.

This third question is a hard one to answer because we are so self-focused. We put *our* priorities first, *our* dreams first, *our* desires first, *our* plans first.

- If you are not able to say yes to this question, repent of your selfishness.

- Ask the Spirit to give you an awareness of others' needs and how to serve others around you.

Question 4:
Do you want to conquer the flesh when you are tempted?

But I say, walk by the Spirit, and you will not gratify the desires of the flesh. For the desires of the flesh are against the Spirit, and the desires of the Spirit are against the flesh, for these are opposed to each other, to keep you from doing the thing you want to do.
GALATIANS 5:16-17

Do you feel this battle? I do, every stinkin' day! We allow the external to affect the internal, rather than the internal to affect the external. We allow ourselves to be controlled by our circumstances rather than by the Spirit within us. Walking by the Spirit does not end the temptations of the flesh, but it can help you overcome these temptations.

We can look at temptation this way: When we are tempted and say no, we are taking steps toward holiness and building our character. When we are tempted and give in, we are taking steps toward our destruction. There is no promise that on this side of heaven we will no longer desire what our flesh desires, but we do not need to live in defeat! If you want to conquer the flesh, ask the Spirit to give you His power to say no to the temptations around you.

Question 5:
Are you willing to receive God's forgiveness and grace for your past in order to embrace what He has for you in the future as you follow Him?

But if you are led by the Spirit, you are not under the law.
GALATIANS 5:18

This is what Shannon didn't grasp. She didn't understand that God's grace was for her. She was no longer under the expectation to be perfect in every area of her life for God to accept her. Overwhelmed by shame, she wouldn't turn to God to be led out of her sin by the power of the Spirit. Unfortunately, this lack of repentance is what caused her to continue to feel disconnected with God. Her fellowship was broken, even if the relationship wasn't.

Scripture teaches, "There is therefore now [not in the future, but now . . .] no condemnation [none at all!] for those who are in Christ Jesus" (Rom. 8:1, brackets added). Christians cannot be condemned, even when we sin, because Christ's righteousness covers us, which means that we are seen as perfect before God. When we truly grasp that there is no condemnation, we can humbly receive God's grace and agree by confessing to God about our sin, and ask for His Spirit to fill us. Then we can walk intimately with Him, and the fellowship is restored.

- If your answer to this question is yes, thank God now for His mercy and grace toward you and that you are no longer under the law that condemns.

- If your answer is no, what is holding you back from receiving His forgiveness and grace?

Question #6:
Do you want the Holy Spirit to transform your life? (Consider which "works of the flesh" listed in Galatians 5:19-20 you may resonate with, even as a believer.)

Now the works of the flesh are evident: sexual immorality, impurity, sensuality, idolatry, sorcery, enmity, strife, jealousy, fits of anger, rivalries, dissensions, divisions, envy, drunkenness, orgies, and things like these.
GALATIANS 5:19-20

It saddens me to see how many people who have a relationship with God are stuck in addiction in the areas of pornography, gossip, a critical spirit, bitterness, image management, disrespect of authority, and the like. They have accepted Jesus into their lives as Savior, they may even want Him to be Lord, but they have not learned how that relationship can actually transform their lives.

Maybe, if you're honest, like Shannon, you don't want this transformation right now. If there is no conviction of the abovementioned sins, then Paul goes on to warn us in Galatians 5:21 about the consequences.

Question 7:
Do you want to experience your true purpose in life?

I warn you, as I warned you before, that those who do such things will not inherit the kingdom of God.
GALATIANS 5:21

This verse might sound extreme, but we cannot ignore it. If we continue to walk in the flesh, ignoring in rebellion the conviction of the Holy Spirit in our lives, we cannot say we are *followers* of Jesus. We might know about Jesus, we might even say we believe in Jesus, but the Bible says that even demons believe and shudder. Just knowing about Jesus and saying He is the Truth isn't what transforms our lives.

If we want to live a victorious life, then we must walk in the power of the Holy Spirit. Without the Holy Spirit, we cannot follow Jesus; we can only know about Him. Without the Holy Spirit, we cannot overcome the addictions in our lives. Without the Holy Spirit, we cannot care about others. Without the Holy Spirit, we will never experience our true purpose in life.

Our purpose is to glorify God the Father, and we do that by bearing much fruit. Jesus said, "By this my Father is glorified, that you bear much fruit and so prove to be my disciples" (John 15:8). We prove that we are His disciples, or followers, by bearing fruit. What is this fruit?

Back to our Galatians passage: "But the fruit of the Spirit is love, joy, peace, patience, kindness, goodness, faithfulness, gentleness, self-control; against such things there is no law" (Gal. 5:22-23). Can you imagine what our lives would look like if we lived out those qualities every day—with everyone? We would change! Our families would change! Our neighbors would change! This world would change!

I CAN'T, BUT, JESUS, YOU CAN

*And those who belong to Christ Jesus have crucified
the flesh with its passions and desires.*
GALATIANS 5:24

If you thought about them deeply and said yes to the seven questions, then you are ready to learn the profound, yet simple, answer to this question: *How do I "crucify" my fleshly passions and desires?*

You say to Jesus, "I can't, but You can. Give me the power that comes from Your Spirit so that I can say yes to righteousness and no to the flesh; so that I can live out the fruit of the Spirit and not the fruit of the flesh. Thank You for giving me the same power that raised You from the dead so that I can live a victorious life and truly walk with You."

There is a spiritual exercise called "spiritual breathing" that helps us apply this to our lives daily. First, we must "exhale" our sin by confessing it to the Lord and repenting, wanting in our hearts to turn from any passion, desire or action that is not pleasing to Him. We admit that, in our own strength, we cannot say no to our flesh.

Then we "inhale" by asking for the power of the Spirit to fill us so that with His strength we can say no to the flesh. We ask the Spirit to focus our passions and desires on God and on His goodness and His love for us.

This simple exercise of spiritual breathing can help you obey the Lord moment by moment when you ask the Spirit to fill you. God's Word assures you that if you ask the Spirit to fill you, He will:

> And I tell you, ask, and it will be given to you; seek, and you will find; knock, and it will be opened to you. For everyone who asks receives, and the one who seeks finds, and to the one who knocks, it will be opened. What father among you, if his son asks for a fish, will instead of a fish give him a serpent; or if he asks for an egg, will give him a scorpion? If you then, who are evil, know how to give good gifts to your children, how much more will your heavenly Father give the Holy Spirit to those who ask him! (Luke 11:9-13).

At any moment, you simply need to ask and the Holy Spirit will empower you! Here is what happens when you ask to be filled with the Spirit: You become dependent on Him to overcome the flesh; and when you overcome the flesh, you experience freedom;

and when you experience freedom, temptation is less enticing; and when temptation is less enticing, you obey more and become more like Jesus!

LIVE BY THE SPIRIT

If we live by the Spirit, let us also keep in step with the Spirit.
GALATIANS 5:25

This is how we are supposed to live. What if only one thing mattered? What if Jesus gave us only one requirement, not a million rules? What if He only asked, "Live by the Spirit, being dependent on Me"? We would then have the power to say no to the flesh and yes to the amazing adventure the Lord has for us!

May each of us walk not just in freedom from sin but also in the power of the Spirit so that we can see our lives and the lives around us changed.

Conversation with God

Take time to pray and ask God the Father to fill you with the Spirit He's already placed inside of you. Here's a suggested prayer: "Dear Father, I need You. I acknowledge that I have been directing my own life and that, as a result, I have sinned against You. I thank You that You have forgiven my sins through Christ's death on the cross for me. I now invite Christ to again take His place on the throne of my life. Fill me with the Holy Spirit as You commanded me to be filled, and as You promised in your Word that You would do if I asked in faith. I now thank You for directing my life and for filling me with the Holy Spirit."

Chapter 11

Follow His Lead into Service

Ministry simply means to serve others as the Lord would have us do—as He did: "For even the Son of Man came not to be served but to serve, and to give his life as a ransom for many" (Mark 10:45). If Jesus came to serve, then we are called to serve, even if we aren't called into vocational ministry. Challenges will arise, as well as blessings, when we follow the Spirit's leading to minister to others. In the book of Acts, we see many scenarios of people who were filled with the Spirit. Let's look at five of those people and see how they can relate to our own desire to walk in the Spirit as we minister to others.

Spirit-filled Servants

No matter what our role is in the Body of Christ, we are all called to serve in the power and direction of the Spirit. In Acts 6, we see that this was true for both appointed leaders and those who were chosen to serve under them. There was a need that had to be filled: widows were being neglected when food was distributed to the poor. To help care for the widows' needs, the 12 apostles were instructed, "Pick out from among you seven men of good repute, full of the Spirit and of wisdom, who we will appoint to this duty" (Acts 6:3). We see here that one of the characteristics to be chosen to serve was to be filled with the Spirit.

It goes on to say that they chose Stephen to oversee these men because he was "full of faith and of the Holy Spirit" (v. 5). So, both the chosen servants and their leader were to have one requirement that was the same: to be filled with the Spirit. It doesn't matter if we see ourselves as leaders or behind-the-scene servants; God calls us to be filled with the Spirit when we serve Him.

IF WE WANT THE HOLY SPIRIT TO USE US MIGHTILY, WE MUST HEAR WHERE HE IS CALLING US TO SERVE AND FOLLOW HIM INTO IT. IN WHAT AREA MIGHT THE SPIRIT BE CALLING YOU TO SERVE?

What's encouraging to know is how others are blessed and ministered to when we serve in the power of the Spirit. Look at the result: "Stephen, full of grace and power [from the Spirit], was doing great wonders and signs among the people" (v. 8). God was using him mightily to impact the people around him!

Stiff-necked People

Not everyone responded positively to Stephen's influence among the people. Some people rose up against Stephen because "they could not withstand the wisdom and the Spirit with which he was speaking" (v. 10). They were against Stephen and his leadership, even though they couldn't deny the Spirit of God speaking through him: "And gazing at him, all who sat in the council saw that his face was like the face of an angel" (v. 15).

Stephen's response was not to get angry or frustrated, but to stand up before this council and share the story of the gospel, starting with Abraham all the way through to Jesus. There were many things he could have pointed out regarding his audience of learned men and religious leaders: their rebellion, their lack of faith, their sin, their pride, their unteachable hearts; but at the end of the narrative, he chose to focus on only one thing: "You stiff-necked people, uncircumcised in heart and ears, you always resist the Holy Spirit" (7:51). His strongest point of contention with them was their resistance to the Holy Spirit in their lives.

IF WE WANT TO BE FILLED WITH THE SPIRIT, WE CANNOT BE STIFF-NECKED PEOPLE. ARE YOU RESISTING THE HOLY SPIRIT IN YOUR LIFE IN SOME WAY? IF SO, WHY? ARE YOU TEACHABLE TO THE FEEDBACK OF OTHER BELIEVERS?

Sometimes we, too, can listen to people speak truth to us, knowing it is the Spirit speaking through them, and we continue to ignore it or we get mad at them because they have exposed a part of our lives where we are not walking with Jesus. The Spirit cannot fill us when we rebel against His instruction. If we want to serve the Lord, we must have a teachable heart to the Spirit as well as to the constructive feedback of other believers.

Persecution

The whole book of Acts was written to inspire us to take steps of faith to share the gospel in order to see lives changed. But that isn't always the result. Stephen took a step of faith to share the gospel in the power of the Spirit and he was stoned to death. But even in that horrific ending, he was filled with the Spirit. "But he, full of the Holy Spirit, gazed into heaven and saw the glory of God, and Jesus standing at the right hand of God" (Acts 7:55). Being filled with the Spirit isn't a promise that we won't be persecuted for our faith, but it can help us see Jesus in the midst of our persecution.

Stephen said these Christlike words as his death drew near: "Lord, do not hold this sin against them" (Acts 7:60). Just like Jesus on the cross, Stephen forgave his persecutors, even though they were killing him. He had a right to be angry at those who were taking his life; instead, he chose to be like Christ and, in the strength of the Spirit, he forgave them. And like Paul, he understood that "to live is Christ, and to die is gain" (Phil. 1:21).

Too often, we hold bitterness in our hearts toward others who have wronged us. We hold on to our "rights." We say that someone has done too great a thing against us to deserve our forgiveness. Yet, here is Stephen, our example. They *stoned* him to death, and he forgave them *while he was being stoned.* How was he able to do that? He was filled with the Spirit.

We can handle persecution and forgive when we are filled with the Spirit. So often we simply pray for God to change our hearts toward others, but we forget that we cannot change without the power of the Spirit.

IF WE WANT TO BE FILLED WITH THE SPIRIT, WE MUST BE WILLING TO ACCEPT PERSECUTION. ARE YOU WILLING TO BE PERSECUTED? ARE YOU WILLING TO FORGIVE OTHERS WHO HAVE WRONGED YOU?

Stephen's ministry began with the Spirit and ended with the Spirit. Let our service be the same.

Power Hungry

As we begin to see the Spirit work in our lives, the temptation will arise in us to try to take on the role of the Holy Spirit and be independent of Him and His power. We get a taste of what it's like to be filled with the Spirit and the power that it brings, and then we try to re-enact it on our own. We begin to believe the lie that we are self-sufficient in impacting others' lives. Or, we might observe how God is using others in the power of the Spirit, and we start to compare or get jealous and demand the same experiences for ourselves.

This is what happened to Simon the magician when he saw the evidence of the Spirit in Philip (see Acts 8). Simon was known for his magic throughout Samaria, and he had a great following. That remained true until Philip came to town telling people about the kingdom of God, and the power of the Holy Spirit started to change lives. Simon saw these great miracles and believed that God was behind them, but he also became envious of this power and wanted to get hold of it himself: "Now when Simon saw that the Spirit was given through the laying on of the apostles hands, he offered them money, saying, 'Give me this power also, so that anyone on whom I lay my hands may receive the Holy Spirit'" (Acts 8:18-19).

Peter saw right through Simon the magician's motives and said, "You have neither part nor lot in this matter, for your heart is not right before God. Repent, therefore, of this wickedness of yours, and pray to the Lord that, if possible, the intent of your heart may be forgiven you. For I see you are in the gall of bitterness and in the bond of iniquity" (vv. 21-23). Peter saw that Simon's main desire was not to make God's name great with this power, but to make his own name great by appearing powerful.

IF WE WANT TO BE FILLED WITH THE SPIRIT, WE MUST CHECK OUR MOTIVES. WHY DO YOU WANT TO BE FILLED WITH THE HOLY SPIRIT?

The Spirit does not give us His power to make our names great. He wants to use us to bring glory to God the Father, not ourselves.

Promptings Led by the Spirit

If we want to be filled with the Spirit so that the Lord can use us to share Jesus with others, we must be willing to *go* where He wants us to go, *when* He wants us to go, and *say* what He wants us to say. We see this exact scenario with Philip in Acts 8:26. He was told by an angel of the Lord to go to Gaza. He wasn't told why, and he didn't ask. He just trusted and went.

As he was on his journey to Gaza, Philip saw a chariot. He didn't know who was in it or why it was stopped on the side of the road, but the Spirit said to him, "Go over and join this chariot" (v. 29). Without knowing what or who he would find, he *ran* to the chariot!

What would you do if you felt God was calling you to go over and talk to someone across the street or in line at the grocery store? Would you do it? What would your response be? It humbles me to read that when Philip heard the voice of the Lord, his response was to run toward where God said to go. He had no clue what to expect, but he ran with great trust and anticipation toward the unknown.

As Philip approached the chariot, he heard a man reading from the book of Isaiah. After greeting the Ethiopian eunuch sitting inside the chariot, Philip asked him if he understood what he was reading. When the Ethiopian admitted that he didn't, Philip saw this as an opportunity to explain the Scriptures. As a result, the Ethiopian put his faith in Christ.

IF WE WANT TO BE USED BY THE HOLY SPIRIT, WE MUST BE SENSITIVE TO HIS GUIDANCE. WHAT DIVINE OPPORTUNITIES MIGHT YOU BE MISSING OUT ON BECAUSE YOU AREN'T FOLLOWING THE DIRECTIONS OF THE SPIRIT?

Philip would have missed out on this amazing encounter if he hadn't obeyed the Spirit by going to Gaza and engaging with the Ethiopian. So much of being filled with the Spirit means hearing the small voice to go talk to someone, to go minister to someone, to go take that crazy step of faith when you don't have all the details figured out.

Preach About the Spirit

Saul was radically changed, and struck blind, when he encountered Jesus on the road to Damascus. Previously, he had been a killer of

Christians, but now Saul was a new convert, and he did not know what he was to do next. That's when Ananias approached him and said, "The Lord Jesus who appeared to you on the road by which you came has sent me so that you may regain your sight and be filled with the Holy Spirit" (Acts 9:17). One of the most important teachings Ananias could give this new convert was an understanding on how to be filled with the Spirit.

How often do you hear teachings on how to be filled with the Spirit? How many people have gone to church and never truly grasped the power that comes from the Spirit? This is one of the most fundamental doctrines to grasp and share with new believers and mature believers alike if we are to see our lives and the lives around us transformed.

Without the Spirit, how can we effectively preach Jesus to one person, or to the masses? The Holy Spirit was given to Paul so that he could have an effective ministry. The Holy Spirit has been given to us. We cannot just make the Spirit-filled life a lesson we teach once and then move on; it is the foundation of discipling people.

IF WE WANT TO SEE THE CHURCH GROW, WE MUST
TEACH OTHERS ABOUT THE SPIRIT-FILLED LIFE.
ARE YOU WILLING TO SHARE THIS WITH OTHERS?
WHERE MIGHT YOU BEGIN SHARING THIS?

When we are filled with the Spirit, we begin to want to tell others about Jesus. Jesus opened Paul's physical eyes, and the Spirit opened his spiritual eyes. One of the first things Paul did afterward was to preach about Jesus. As a result, the Church began to grow numerically and in understanding: "So the church throughout all Judea and Galilee and Samaria had peace and was being built up. And walking in the fear of the Lord and in the comfort of the Holy Spirit, it multiplied" (Acts 9:31).

Not only was Paul filled with the Spirit, but the people that comprised the Church were filled with the Spirit as well. The Holy

Spirit was never given just to the leaders or to the spiritually mature; the Holy Spirit was given to every believer the moment that person believed in Jesus; and He wants to work in and through every believer within the Body of Christ.

The Holy Spirit was not only given to us as individuals, but to the entire Church body so that the Church would multiply. How does the Church grow? As we learn to walk in the Spirit, ourselves, we then teach others in the church to do so.

MOMENT OF REFLECTION

- Leaders and servants alike are to be filled with the Spirit as they serve the Lord.

- We can bring glory to God through persecution when we are filled with the Holy Spirit.

- We can forgive those who persecute us, like Stephen did, when we are filled with the Holy Spirit.

- We will know where to go (but maybe not why) when we are filled with the Spirit.

- We can talk to strangers and share the gospel, like Philip did, when we are filled with the Holy Spirit.

- The Holy Spirit is meant for new believers and mature believers alike, to build up the Church and multiply it.

Questions to Ponder

1. Go back to each section of this chapter and reflect on the question in the callout.

2. What is your role in the Body of Christ? Do you know where He wants you to serve? If you are already serving, are you doing so in the power of the Holy Spirit?

3. Do you resist the Holy Spirit in your life? If so, in which areas? Why do you do this?

4. Do you inform people in a loving, grace-filled way when it seems like they are resisting the Holy Spirit? Why is that a loving thing to do?

5. Have you experienced any persecution for your faith? If so, how did you respond? Were you filled with the Spirit?

6. Are there people who have wronged you that you need to forgive in the Spirit? If you hold on to bitterness, the Spirit cannot powerfully use you. What bitterness might you need to confess and repent of?

7. Have there been situations where you've tried to be the Holy Spirit and make things happen in your own strength and timing instead of letting Him lead? What were the results of your taking the lead instead?

8. Why do you want to receive the power of the Spirit? Is it for your own glory or His?

9. Are you willing to go where He wants you to go, even if you don't know why?

10. Is there someone you can share the concept of the Spirit-filled life with who may be struggling in his or her Christian walk, or someone who may want to make an impact for Christ but isn't sure how to go about it?

Conversation with God

1. Ask God to show you where and how He'd like you to serve and minister to others.

2. Ask God to reveal to you if you have resisted the Holy Spirit in your life. Ask God to reveal to you if you have unforgiveness or bitterness in your heart. Confess and repent of these things and thank Him for forgiving you and giving you a clean slate to move forward with Him.

3. Ask for God to be glorified in your life so that you would not be the one being recognized for your "good deeds" but that He would be acknowledged for His powerful work in others through you.

4. Pray for God to reveal to you which friends you should share the concept of the Spirit-filled life with. Then ask Him to give you clarity to share what you've learned and applied in your own life through following Him.

Chapter 12

Follow His Lead Through Surrender

Following the Holy Spirit's lead requires surrender. In the moment, surrender can feel like a devastating loss, like a seemingly endless pit in the stomach and a battle for our deepest longings and dreams. It's hard to see past our immediate wants and desires to believe that there is a better life, if we choose to trust, obey and surrender.

When it comes to moments of surrender, there is another way we can look at it besides what we are leaving behind. We can look at the possibilities and cling to the hope of entering into God-sized adventures that are just a few steps of faith ahead.

What adventures might be waiting for you just by asking the Spirit to empower you daily? To say, "Lord, I surrender. I'm sad to let these things go, but I want to choose to trust that Your plans are better. I will walk by faith where You lead me."

We are not our own. We were bought with a price. And with that price also came a gift. The Holy Spirit came to reside in us so that we would have the ability to surrender and live a life that is glorifying to God: "Or do you not know that your body is a temple of the Holy Spirit within you, whom you have from God? You are not your own, for you were bought with a price. So glorify God in your body" (1 Cor. 6:19-20).

A surrendered life doesn't just happen once and that's it. Jesus said, "If anyone would come after me, let him deny himself and take up his cross daily and follow me" (Luke 9:23). It's not a recommitment, but a daily giving over of our self: our thoughts, desires, dreams and actions, to the one who created us for a greater purpose than ourselves. It is about following Him into the unknown, not just living by the book. Are you willing to surrender control of your thoughts, desires, dreams and actions? Are you willing to follow Him into the unknown and see His vision for your life?

If so, then practice giving yourself to the Lord each day. Pray through your day and what you have planned to accomplish. Then surrender your plans and their results to Him. Admit where you are not strong and need His strength to persevere. Admit where you are tempted, and ask for the Spirit's power to conquer that temptation. Ask for the Spirit to center your focus on others so that He can use you in the lives of others. Then, listen for His voice, stand back and see what happens!

Here's a humbling thought when it comes to wanting our lives to glorify God and make an impact: *What if you could only count the moments of your life when you were filled with the Holy Spirit?* How many days would count? Alternatively, how many days will be consumed by God's righteous fire due to their lack of being lived with God? How much of your days, weeks and years are counting for the Lord because it was His Spirit living in and through you? It can be a sobering thought, but hopefully it will motivate you to begin living the Christian life differently.

Remember this: How long you've been a believer isn't what matters; what matters is how you live your life after you become a believer.

The Pledge

So what is God asking of you? What does it look like to daily surrender to Him? Dr. Bill Bright, the founder of Campus Crusade for Christ, wrote a pledge to the Lord when he and his wife, Vonette, felt called to start this mission's organization. He knew that without a surrendered life, the Lord could not powerfully use him. Sixty years later, a new pledge of surrender has been written to encourage believers to live surrendered lives:

> *Lord Jesus, I surrender to You. In the power of Your Spirit, I*
> *will . . .*
> *GO where You want me to go,*
> *DO what You want me to do,*
> *SAY what You want me to say,*
> *GIVE what You want me to give.*

Though simple, signing a pledge like this one had a profound effect on this couple's life as they daily committed to walk in the power of the Holy Spirit in order to impact this world for Christ.

On September 23, 2012, my husband, Matt, and I made this pledge to the Lord on our wedding day. Alongside of our vows, we wanted to dedicate our lives and marriage to the Lord's work. We had 15 pastors, who had impacted our lives throughout the years, lay hands on us and pray for us as we were commissioned to go where God wanted us to go; do what God wanted us to do; say what God wanted us to say; and give what God wanted us to give.

Go

Going where He wants me to go hasn't always been easy. In some ways, I'm used to "going" as I've traveled to 27 countries while serving the Lord in vocational ministry. Yet, there are times when going can still be a challenge, like when He asked me to pack up my things when I lived in Berkeley and head overseas. I didn't know if I'd come back.

After serving at UC Berkeley for five years with Cru, I knew it was time to serve Him for a season overseas. *My* plan was to go for one year and then come back to serve at UC Berkeley again; but God had other plans. God knew I wouldn't be going back there, but I didn't. My battle with the Lord wasn't about going overseas, but about surrendering my apartment that I thought I would come back to.

My plan also entailed keeping the five students I had recruited to go with me on my team. But that wasn't God's plan either. We needed two teams in East Asia, so we were asked to pray about splitting up. We were extremely disappointed that we wouldn't be able to serve together, but we knew it was what the Lord was calling us to do.

If I didn't choose to surrender even the little things, I knew I would begin my year with bitterness, disappointment and hurt. Sometimes, before we obey the Spirit's leading to go, we need to grieve what we are leaving behind and let go of the things we hoped to hold on to in the transition.

One month before we left, I wrote this poem of surrender in my journal. It was written with tears and grief. Now, years later, I see that the things I gave up were so small compared to what I received by following His lead.

Surrender
May 2004

Oh, Lord,
You're asking me to surrender.
It feels as if the muscles are being pulled from my bone.
Everything of appearing significance will be taken away.
Can my heart handle it?
Am I strong enough?
You pluck them from my grasp—
Things that brought joy, comfort, purpose.
Things I never thought I'd be able to surrender.

The Lord said,
"Surrender your home.
Offer it to others.
To those who may
not even be thankful.
Who may think they deserve it.

Holly A. Melton

Offer it to them anyways.
Bless them in a way they've never been blessed.
Show them love that they've never seen expressed."

Lord, I surrender . . .
My home.
A place of peace, comfort and community.
Greatly cherished.
Offered to another.
In the blessing, I was blessed.
There was great joy in the offering.

Then the Lord said,
"Surrender your team.
You thought you'd lead.
You thought you'd all go together.
One by one, they went elsewhere.
And then there were three.
Yet another challenge:
One woman is needed to go elsewhere.
Will you be the one?
Surrender the team, the city. Will you still go?"

Lord, I surrender . . .
My dreams of a partnership.
I will go alone.
Surprise blessing: One will go with me.
Someone I know and who knows me.

Then the Lord said,
"Surrender your role at Cal.
You will not be going back.
Carla and Brad need to lead together; without you.
You will leave a great working relationship.
You will leave four new staff women.
You will leave the intern you led to the Lord."

Lord, I surrender.
Peace floods my soul.
I hear, "Well done, good and faithful servant."
What a blessing . . . and I let go.

Then the Lord said,
"Take care of yourself.
Don't lead the team.
Learn the language.
Serve and be served.
Six months just be a team member."

Lord, I surrender.
It's challenging.
It's good.
It's a blessing.

Then the Lord said,
"Surrender your finances.
Let go of your safety net.
Have integrity.
Don't raise support for East Asia.
Grow your faith.
Give it all away.
Go, trusting I will provide."

Lord, I surrender my finances . . .
I receive deep joy in giving and blessing others.
Then the Lord said,
"Surrender your future after East Asia."

But, Lord,
It feels like a big black hole.
Nothing excites me.

The Lord said,
"Think 'new horizon' . . . not yet painted.
Get excited."

Holly A. Melton

Lord, I surrender not knowing . . .
I experience Your presence, purpose and peace.

Surrender.
It's about God's will, not mine.
There I've found peace, comfort, faith,
    purpose, strength and blessing.
Yes, even hints of joy.
I *will* surrender.

Do

Doing what He wants me to do isn't always easy. Even though I have served in the church in some capacity since I was a youth, certain things are still outside of my comfort zone. Interacting with the homeless was one of them. Until I lived in Berkeley, I hadn't lived in a city where I saw many homeless, let alone engaged with them in conversation.

This all changed when Ken, a homeless man who lived in Berkeley's infamous People's Park, started to attend our church each week. Ken was a very relational man in his mid-50s, and hungry to study God's Word. He wanted to join a small group but had no way of getting there by public transit. One of my friends who drove with me to small group suggested we offer to pick him up and have him join us.

The car rides to and from small group were always filled with delightful and insightful conversation. I learned from Ken that one of the reasons it's so hard to get off the streets once people are homeless is that most employers want them to have a permanent address before they are accepted as an employee. Obviously, homeless people don't have a permanent address. This creates an enormous challenge for many of them to get off the streets.

One evening on the drive home from small group, I felt the clear prodding of the Holy Spirit to *do* something about Ken's situation. I knew some might disagree with what I was going to offer, but I just felt in my spirit that this is what I was supposed to ask. I took a deep breath and blurted out, "Ken, would you like to live in my apartment this summer while I'm gone? It will be vacant for two months, and I thought maybe you'd like to stay there until I return."

My heart pounded as I waited for his answer. I didn't want him to feel uncomfortable or insulted with my request. He looked at me in shock, and said, "Holly! Are you serious? This would give me a chance to get a job and get off the streets. Yes! Yes!"

Those two months were significant in Ken's life. Though he had a roof over his head, he did not forget his friends at People's Park. Every Sunday afternoon he'd bring them peanut butter and jelly sandwiches, which they would eat together while he'd teach them whatever he'd learned that morning at church. Eventually, Ken officially started a church for the homeless.

When I returned, after two months away, Ken was no longer homeless. He had secured a job and saved enough money in those two months to move into his own apartment. But what he was most excited to share with me was how the Lord was now calling him to missions in Africa! I couldn't believe how much his life had changed in just two months. I had no clue that doing what the Lord wanted me to do in offering my vacant apartment to a homeless man would bear so much fruit!

Say

Saying what the Holy Spirit wants me to say isn't always easy. At times, I don't want to say what He puts on my heart to encourage or exhort a person around me, because it seems like it would just take too much emotional energy and time.

There's no guarantee how a person will receive what you are called to say, but you can have peace in knowing the rest is in God's hands to orchestrate in the person's life.

This is what happened in my early 20s when the Holy Spirit wanted me to exhort a woman who was at least twice my age. Though highly respected by many people, if you were to spend time with her, she would gossip about others and label them based on areas they needed to grow in. For example, she might say, "George, the workaholic . . . Peter, the conflict-avoider . . . Marsha, the verbally aggressive . . ."

She was in a position of leadership and influence, but her labels of people were coming across as disrespectful and judgmental. I felt the Holy Spirit encourage me to gently reflect to her my experience of how she talked about people "in light of their development." Though I tried to listen, learn and reflect back what I heard, after six hours of dialogue with her, we were still in disagreement on whether it was appropriate or not to discuss others' growth areas so openly.

There are times, even in the Body of Christ, when things stay unreconciled. The Lord desires us to be right with everyone, as much as it depends on us, but it takes two people for reconciliation to happen.

It was five years later when the Holy Spirit put this woman on my heart again. I was taking a leadership class, and the instructor asked us to write down leaders who have influenced us to be the person we are today. Her name quickly came to my mind because she had mentored me through some difficult situations and, ironically, had taught me how to speak the truth in love to others.

After we wrote down the names of leaders who had influenced us, the teacher suggested we think of some way to thank these people for their influence in our lives. Immediately, the thought came to me to send her flowers. My flesh fought back and argued, "Why waste money on sending her flowers when you aren't even reconciled?" That was exactly why I knew I needed to do it.

I didn't hear from her after the flowers were delivered, but I did see her at an event about a week later. I knew it would negate my purpose in sending her the flowers of appreciation if I did not approach her and thank her personally. Unfortunately, when I did so, the conversation was not so pleasant. I left the room wanting to cry with grief. The Lord comforted me with His presence and reassured me that I had said what He wanted me to say and done what He wanted me to do and given what He wanted me to give; the rest would be between Him and her.

As I reflect back on that situation, I am so thankful I said what the Lord wanted me to say. Even though it was one of the more painful relationships in my life, the Spirit used it to develop me and, I hope, one day her as well.

Give

Giving what He wants me to give isn't always easy. He wants me to give my time, my talents and my treasure. He wants me to give all of my finances to Him to use as He wants it to be used. This means giving money to my friends for their adoption or for a surgery; or giving for a child to have food, medical attention and good schooling in a foreign country; or giving to students going on mission trips for the first time. It means giving cheerfully to anything He asks me to give to.

I have lived on the personal financial support of others for the past 14 years of my life. Receiving people's hard-earned money for me to live and serve in vocational ministry is a humbling experience. There are many opinions as to whether Christians should live as if they are in poverty or just give their 10 percent to the church or, at the very least, donate to charities around Christmas time.

My entire perspective on giving changed when I decided to see my banking account as "God's bank" and not create rules or expectations on where I give or how much. I would tell those who support me that they were entrusting me with their money to use as the Lord guides me.

Being "God's banker" has been a very fun and encouraging role to play. I truly believe that we cannot outgive God. Over and over again, I have given by faith and seen the Lord provide for me when I chose to sacrificially give to others. Yet, it is those who have given sacrificially to *me* that spur me on the most.

One of the most humble givers I know is a man who is only in his mid-thirties, but is a retired vet from military service. He came home from serving our country and was diagnosed with post-traumatic stress disorder, as well as being bi-polar. He is very shy, and has a nervous twitch and stutter. This hinders him from getting out much. He is unemployed due to his mental and emotional state, but he receives a disability check each month for his income. Despite his physical and mental challenges, this man loves Jesus and wants to live with eternity in mind. One way he saw he could do that is with his meager finances. Each month he would sacrificially give me $400 toward my ministry needs. He was clearly my largest ministry supporter.

Sitting face to face with him one day, I asked him why he gave so much when he had so little. Barely able to make eye contact with me, he said, "I know I am too messed up to make a significant impact on this earth, but I know I can invest in you, and that way I will have a significant impact on eternity." I left our time together with a heavy, humbled heart. To give to God when He asks us to give is one of the most significant things we can do this side of heaven. I love that my friend saw that, and I was humbled to be the recipient of his sacrificial gift.

You Only Live Once

We won't be able to *go* where He wants us to go or *do* what He wants us to do or *say* what He wants us to say or *give* what He wants us to give if we aren't following His lead and walking in the power of the Holy Spirit. Without the Holy Spirit, we cannot live a surrendered life and walk in the will of the Father. But *with* the Holy Spirit, we can engage in each of these things through His direction and power. As a result, our lives will have an eternal impact on those around us.

I'm closing this chapter, and book, by sharing the story of my friend Monique. She had cystic fibrosis and passed away the day after her thirty-fourth birthday. She lived her life in hospitals, but she also lived a life of faith. She saw each day she was given as precious.

When she was 28, she needed a double lung transplant. When lungs were finally available for her, she wrestled with the question of whether she should receive these lungs or let the next person on the list have them. When discussing this decision with our pastor, her ultimate concern was, "What if the person after me on the list doesn't know Jesus and then *he or she* dies, and *I* live? I would rather be with Jesus now than have that happen." Somehow, my pastor helped her see that these lungs were a gift for her to elongate her days on this earth; and she, in faith, received this as a blessing from the Lord and had the surgery. God ordained her to live six more years, until November 23, 2010.

What is also so beautiful about her story was that Monique had the dream of getting married, even though she knew she probably would not live a long life. She resolved to trust the Lord if she were to stay single, but she continued to pray that the Lord would bring a godly man into her life.

God brought Shay into her life through an Internet dating site, and they quickly grew to love each other. Our pastor warned Shay that Monique may not live for very long, but Shay said he would trust God through it.

Monique and Shay were married, and they lived most of their marriage with Monique in hospitals. They celebrated each month of their marriage. Ten months after they wed, Shay's bride went to be with her other bridegroom, Jesus. Here are the words Shay emailed to some friends at 6:54 AM, the morning they knew she was going to pass away:

Monique was special. We all loved her and were able to see the way she lived for Jesus day in and day out. What a great example. She affected everyone she came in contact with. Earlier today, I witnessed an employee here at the hospital who only knew her a few weeks, and she wept as she said goodbye. You all know she had a way of loving everyone. Too many times to count she met a stranger and walked away with a close friend. She shared Jesus and loved everyone. I am still amazed by the way she was. She would barely be able to breathe, yet ask people how they were doing and how she could pray for them. She cared for others first, just the way we are all supposed to do.

Holly A. Melton

Sometime today she is going to go meet Jesus. This is the moment she has been craving her whole life. She wants nothing more. Too many of us are busy living here. Not Monique; she was living here, but her eyes were focused there. She will be very happy soon. I am happy for her. It will be a hard day for all of the family. Please keep them in prayer.

Some of you will say, "Shay, I am so sorry for you." Don't be. I was the lucky one. I was made by God to love and marry Monique. It was the greatest time of my life. God blessed me in such an amazing way. I found someone special who was made just for me. Every day, every moment, was worth it. Sure I wish I had more time, who wouldn't? But what an amazing time I had. I am so thankful for what Jesus gave me. What gifts my father in heaven saw fit for me. It is humbling, and I can do nothing but praise Him for it.

God made everything, including our beautiful Monique, and we were all blessed to know her. Thank You, Jesus, so much for letting us all know Monique and spend time with her before You took her home. God has been so good to us all.

What a life she lived. One day we will all get to be with her again. Thank You, Jesus, for making a way: eternity with Christ and a chance to hang out with Monique again. She will be there, and I can't wait to see her again. —Shay

Hundreds of mourners packed into the church for Monique's memorial service. Many were people who had been diagnosed with the same disease as she, holding on to their own lives by a thread. Many shared how she had been a comfort, an inspiration and God's encouragement to them in their sickness. Even with an illness that eventually took her life, Monique lived every day in the power of the Holy Spirit and surrendered her entire life, and being, to Him. What if we all chose to see our one life like Monique did?

No matter what circumstances we've been dealt in life, we can still live this life for eternal impact. We can still see our lives become more like Jesus and impact the lives of others as we walk in the Spirit and follow His lead. You only live once. How do *you* want to live your one life?

MOMENT OF REFLECTION

This is not just a book of inspiring stories. These are stories inspired by the Holy Spirit as He worked through moments of human surrender in divine ways to change lives. God is not finished using us to draw people to Himself. We must believe that when we choose to walk in the power of the Holy Spirit, we will see Him transform us and impact the people around us.

The prayer of the apostle Paul recorded in Ephesians 3:14-21 is my prayer for you as *you* now follow His lead.

> For this reason I bow my knees before the Father, from whom every family in heaven and on earth is named, that according to the riches of his glory he may grant you to be strengthened with power through his Spirit in your inner being, so that Christ may dwell in your hearts through faith—that you, being rooted and grounded in love, may have strength to comprehend with all the saints what is the breadth and length and height and depth, and to know the love of Christ that surpasses knowledge, that you may be filled with all the fullness of God. Now to him who is able to do far more abundantly than all that we ask or think, according to the power at work within us, to him be glory in the church and in Christ Jesus throughout all generations, forever and ever. Amen.

May *you* be filled with the Holy Spirit; may *you* know more deeply the love of Christ; may your life be *filled* with all the fullness of God; and may He do *far more abundantly* in your life than you can imagine, as you choose to surrender to Him.

Holly A. Melton

Now it's your turn to follow His lead and see what divine encounters He has waiting for you!

Questions to Ponder

• Is there a memorable time when you did *not* walk in the power of the Holy Spirit? How did that affect you and others?

• Is there a memorable time when you *did* walk in the power of the Holy Spirit? How did that affect you and others?

• Why do you think we tend to not want to walk in the Spirit or are unwilling to surrender to the Spirit, even after having positive outcomes when we do?

• Are you at a place of surrender right now where you are willing to pledge to go, do, say and give whatever the Lord wants? If so, take some time to pledge your surrender and commitment to the Lord.

Conversation with God

The Pledge:

> *Lord Jesus, I surrender to You. In the power of Your Spirit, I will . . .*
> *GO where You want me to go,*
> *DO what You want me to do,*
> *SAY what You want me to say,*
> *GIVE what You want me to give. Amen.*

If you made this pledge to the Lord, sign and date below to remember this day and the commitment you've made to follow His lead wherever He leads you.

Name: _____Date: _____

You can publicly join others in this commitment by going to www.pledge.cru.org and express where the Lord would have you go and what He would have you do, say or give. On that website you will be encouraged to see what others are surrendering to the Lord by faith. The website will also have resources available for you to continue to grow in the area of surrender.

I would love to personally hear from you so that I can encourage you from time to time. Feel free to email me at Holly.Melton@cru.org and let me know if you signed the pledge. I will commit to pray for you to live a surrendered life in the power of the Holy Spirit, and that you would follow Him in your everyday encounters with others.

Holly A. Melton

Acknowledgments

With Deep Gratitude, I Thank . . .

Jon Roper, for casting the vision on a bus in Egypt to write a book so that I can further my desire to speak on the Holy Spirit; Susan Peterson and Robin Garbisch, who edited my first draft and encouraged me that this book is for all ages; for Richard Horn and Chris Gould, for their wisdom with the Scriptures; David Martinelli and Patty McCain, my friends and leaders, for entrusting to me the time I needed to write this book as part of my ministry within Cru; for all the staff in Cru and the students who have asked me to write down these stories so that others can be inspired to walk in the power of the Holy Spirit; for my parents, Wes and Lydia Ashman, who have prayed me into being the woman I am today; for my wonderful husband, Matt Melton, who let me write every morning the first four months of our marriage, and encouraged me every step of the way so that I could finish this book on time; for the Holy Spirit, who has sealed me, filled me and who works in me to become more like Jesus while also empowering me to minister to others. He is truly the greatest gift Jesus could have given me after salvation and God's Word.

Holly A. Melton